THIS BOOK WILL TEACH YOU

# ESSENTIAL SALES STRATEGIES

## THE INSIDER'S GUIDE TO SELLING AND WINNING NEW CUSTOMERS

WHALEN
BOOK·WORKS

*This Book Will Teach You Essential Sales Strategies*

13-digit ISBN: 978-1-95151-112-8
10-digit ISBN: 1-95151-112-8

This book may be ordered by mail from the publisher. Please include $5.99 for postage and handling. Please support your local bookseller first!

Books published by Whalen Book Works are available at special discounts when purchased in bulk. For more information, please email us at info@whalenbookworks.com.

Whalen Book Works
68 North Street
Kennebunkport, ME 04046

www.whalenbookworks.com

Printed in China
1 2 3 4 5 6 7 8 9 0

First Edition

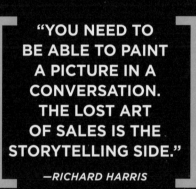

"YOU NEED TO
BE ABLE TO PAINT
A PICTURE IN A
CONVERSATION.
THE LOST ART
OF SALES IS THE
STORYTELLING SIDE."

—RICHARD HARRIS

# CONTENTS

# INTRODUCTION

*This Book Will Teach You Essential Sales Strategies* teaches readers the basics of sales and cultivating and keeping customers. You may be selling a product or service, or you may be "selling" yourself to an interviewer, but having the right mindset from the beginning is crucial to achieving success. This guide will show you how to overcome fears and uncertainties, forge bonds with clients, and become a selling expert!

The book introduces you to the world of sales, one of the key components of most businesses. "Sales" aren't only about products and services; you are "selling" the idea of yourself at an interview or when speaking with a potential client, for example. Within a company framework, sales can be business-to-business (B2B) or business-to-customer (B2C), both of which can be crucial to a thriving, successful company. It can be a massive undertaking or a simple one, but it can feel confusing and overwhelming to both the beginner and also the novice.

Whatever you're selling, establishing the right attitude is essential! If reaching out to others to sell anything petrifies you (not to worry, it does that for many people!), the advice here will help you to overcome that and gain confidence in your selling abilities and what you have to offer. You will also learn about developing good relations with your potential customers, understanding and meeting their needs, why failure isn't always a bad thing, and why closing the deal is only one of the goals of a good sale. With this guide, you'll be able to overcome your doubts and be on your way to mastering the art of selling!

The book is divided into chapters grouped by subject. Each offers important information and gives you a starting point, focusing on simple how-tos to get you started. Use this information as a reference and handy guide when you want to look up something about a specific topic quickly. Dip into the book wherever you like and read it in any order that works for you. Some sections may be more relevant to you than others, but there is something here for everyone who is starting out. A book this size can only give you a brief summary, but you can use it as a jumping-off place for further learning and background research. Remember that this book is not a substitute for legal or other advice, and if you need further help on any of the topics here, you will need to seek it out. The Resources section at the end provides much helpful further reading, and a list of websites will give you more detailed information. Let this book be your introduction to the complex but endlessly fascinating world of selling!

> **"If you are not taking care of your customer, your competitor will."**
>
> **—BOB HOOEY**

[ CHAPTER 1: ]

# WELCOME TO THE WONDERFUL WORLD OF SALES! OH BOY . . .

## WHAT IS SELLING, EXACTLY?

Put simply, selling is a transaction between a seller and a buyer for something that the buyer wants or needs, in exchange for something of value, usually money. The seller is trying to persuade the buyer to part with their money, and the buyer wants to feel as if they are getting their money's worth. Both parties want to come away happy with what they've received. What the buyer is looking for can be a need or a want, or very often a want packaged as a need. It can be something physical, or it can be a service.

# SELLING PRODUCTS VERSUS SELLING SERVICES

Businesses most often sell products or services. But many companies do both. A business that sells a big-screen television that comes with a three-year warranty is giving you both a product and a service. You get the TV (a product), but if anything goes wrong, they pledge to repair it (a service) for the first three years. Or maybe someone sells you a service along with a product. A self-help coach may sell their advice in your ongoing sessions, and also a workbook that you have to read and work through as a part of the program. It's also entirely possible to sell one without the other. A business consultant may be brought in solely to advise on some area in which they have expertise (no product), while a food truck sells you their amazing Mexican cuisine at lunchtime (no service, beyond giving you your lunch).

# OTHER KINDS OF SELLING

In most business environments, these will be the two most common things for sale, but selling occurs in many other ways, too, ones that you may not have thought of. If you are a freelancer, you're selling your limited-time services to a company that hires you for a specific task to be done during a specific time (to design their website or write a technical manual, for example). If you do good work for them, they may "buy" your services again in the future, or they may decide to hire you on permanently. If you're interviewing for a job, you're effectively selling yourself and your experience in the hopes that the company "buys" (i.e., hires) you. If you are a nonprofit or a charity, you may be selling the idea of your work to a sponsor or benefactor. They are "buying" the idea that you're presenting to them and want to give you support to see it come to fruition.

Selling happens on many levels, though it's likely that you're reading this book for advice on the sale of goods and services, so that's where the focus will be.

# TYPES OF MARKETS

Usually, selling can be done to three different markets: consumer, industrial, and reseller.

- **Consumer:** This is the market of the general public, everything from groceries to laptops. These are the everyday people who buy what you're selling.

- **Industrial:** This is the market of people and businesses who buy what you produce to help produce their own products or services, or to run their operations. Everything from tools that mechanics buy to accounting software falls into this category.

- **Reseller:** This is the market of the middlemen, who buy products to resell for a profit. A store buys items from manufacturers (perhaps at discount prices), and then resells them to make its own profit above what the manufacturer gets. Wholesalers buy things in bulk and then resell them at higher than the cost they purchased them for.

It's possible that you'll be selling to more than one market. You might have a baking service that sells to customers out of your shop, but which also provides baked goods to the local grocery stores to resell, for example.

# GREAT SELLERS ARE MADE, NOT BORN

We all know people who just seem to have an inherent talent for something. Maybe they picked up the guitar without having had a lesson in their life; maybe they're a whiz with languages. Yeah, those kinds of people can be annoying. But you also probably have things that you're great at that didn't seem to take much effort to master. And somebody probably resents you for it. But what about sales? Are great salespeople born that way, or do they learn it as they go along? The answer is a definitive yes!

Sorry for that nonresponse, but a lot of experts who weigh in argue for one side or another, which tells you that you can find plenty of examples of both . . . or maybe that the experts are wrong. Sales expert Steve Martin (not the comedian, though wouldn't that be great?) has estimated that about 70 percent of the best salespeople he's seen over the years are "born" with it. What that really means is that they have natural personality traits that contribute to being able to close the deal again and again. However, others strongly disagree with this generalization, arguing that most people learn their sales skills as they develop, even if they showed a talent for it at a young age. So, even someone in their teens who can make a sale has been molded and shaped by their environment and teachers.

What does this debate mean for you? Thankfully, not all that much! You may not feel that you have the qualifications to be a great salesperson, but the good news is that you can learn and improve with practice. That may not help you with your irritating friend who can play every Led Zeppelin song on guitar by ear while you struggle to pick out a few chords, but when it comes to selling, you can and will get better!

# SIX INSIGHTS INTO THE MINDSET AND PRACTICES OF A GREAT SALESPERSON

So how does a master seller think? There are lots of different answers to this question, probably as many as there are great salespeople. Each person will bring their own unique experiences and talents to the table, and the advice of one won't be good for all. Here are some great qualities to keep in mind when you're trying to succeed in sales.

1. **Understand what it is you're selling, inside and out.** If you don't understand it, how will your customer be able to? If you're not even sure if you like it or if it works, why should they be? Beyond knowing these things, why are you selling your product or service in the first place? Who is it for? And just as importantly, who is it **not** for? Knowing your audience is crucial to being able to find your most likely customers. No one sells something that everyone wants, even if it's a basic human need (look how many different brands of bread and milk there are, for example). Narrow your focus and know what you're offering.

2. **Have empathy for your customer.** Being able to put yourself in someone else's shoes is critical to forging a good relationship. Ask questions, listen, and learn. Be aware that they may get frustrated or angry. You need to be able to build trust, one of the key factors in moving toward a successful sale. Price is less of an object if the customer trusts you and you can deliver on what you say. A low price means nothing if they're suspicious of you. Back up everything you say with a guarantee and deliver on it.

3. **Focus on helping your customers, but don't try to sell to them.** Of course, you're trying to sell, but if you come off as trying to sell, you'll likely chase more people away than you keep. You need to know how your product can help someone out, and you should want to help people. There is tremendous satisfaction in reaching out and helping to solve someone's problem or taking care of their needs.

4. **Be patient.** A customer will buy when they are ready. Your goal is to help that process along, but understand that they need to go through the process in their own time. Getting pushy, leaning on them, pressuring them, or any other aggressive tactics are a sure way to ruin the sale, or at the very least, have dissatisfied customers at the end of it. Even if they end up liking the product, they may never come back to you.

5. **Be responsive.** Maybe your sale is simple. But maybe it's a big, complex affair that requires multiple decision-makers before it's complete. If it's a process that goes on for a while (say, over days or weeks), always, *always* get back to your buyer as soon as possible to answer questions, calm concerns, and give extra insight. Whatever their needs are, be sure you are there for them when they ask for you. If you wait days to return their email or call, you'll run the risk of losing the sale. The quickest way to tell a customer you don't care is to ignore them.

6. **Control what you can, and be OK with that.** You can control things on your end, but you can't control how the customer will respond. Things may be going great and then suddenly fall apart. They may change their minds, they may go with a competitor, they may lose interest, or they might decide to wait and think about it before moving forward. And you know what? This is all OK. It happens. You'll lose some sales and you can't control these things. But being confident in everything on your part gives you the best chance of closing the deal.

# FOUR BASIC THEORIES OF SELLING

> There's more to selling than just making a pitch and collecting the money! There are many different business, scientific, and psychological models for how and why we buy and sell, but it's useful to understand some of the more common theories to get a little information on how to make your sales more effective. Here are some of the more common ones, and each is worth studying in more detail. You'll gain valuable insights that will help you later on.

1. **AIDAS Theory:** AIDAS stands for attention, interest, desire, action, and satisfaction. These five stages are crucial to the sale, and a potential customer will go through all five before finally committing to buy. It's therefore necessary to make sure that you guide the customer through each stage.

   - **Attention:** How do you attract someone's attention? You need to do it without attempting a hard sell. Start a conversation.

   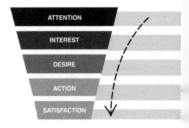

   - **Interest:** Can you maintain a potential customer's interest, or will they get bored and move on?

   - **Desire:** You need to be able to instill a desire for the product or service—not just a want but a need to buy it, and the sooner the better.

   - **Action:** Desire to buy doesn't always equal an immediate purchase. What can you do to help that customer take immediate action?

- **Satisfaction:** The customer has to be happy with their purchase after the sale. You need to ensure that they are satisfied and have made the right choice, a choice that was theirs, not one that you pressured them into.

2. **Situation-Response Theory:** Also known as the "Right Set of Circumstances" theory, this model involves putting everything together to create just the right circumstances for a customer to say yes. The seller controls this process and tries to make the sale as perfect as possible for the buyer, who will then react in a predictable way (hopefully the way you want!).

3. **Product-Oriented Theory:** This theory assumes that a customer is new to your product or service and needs to be educated about its benefits to them. Of course, the seller has to understand the product and the needs of the potential customer, so that they can show how the benefits match what the buyer needs.

4. **Behavior Equation Theory:** This theory focuses on the buyer's needs and tries to satisfy them. In short, the equation says that $B=PDKV$, where B is the buyer's response, P is how they are predisposed to respond, D is the drive they have to buy, K is the perceived value of the product, and V is how intense the triggers and stimuli are to making their decision. All of these factors will influence whether or not you make the sale.

> **"Don't find customers for your products, find products for your customers."**
>
> **—SETH GODIN**

# WHAT ARE YOU SELLING? AND OTHER QUESTIONS BEFORE YOU BEGIN

This may seem like a ridiculous question, but you have to ask it of yourself. In fact, you'll need to ask a lot of questions when you begin the process.

- **What is your product or service?** Define it, not just for your customers but for yourself. If you don't know the product inside and out, how can anyone trust you?

- **Who is it for?** Who's going to want what you sell? Who's going to need it? Do those two things overlap? You must have the right target audiences, and you need to narrow them down. "This product is for everyone" is never the case. It just isn't. Some people will need it more than others, so who are they? Get narrow and get focused. A loyal customer base of a few hundred is a better start that an uncommitted group of a thousand who may or may not ever buy.

- **Why you and why now?** What is it about your business that makes you uniquely suited to offer this product? What is your experience and background? How are you qualified? You don't necessarily need to tell prospective customers this info (it might just bore them), but you need to be aware of it for yourself. You are in this business because you think you can offer something great, so be sure you can back up that claim. Also, why is your product needed right now? What's the urgency?

- **What is the benefit?** What specifically is this product or service bringing to the world? It could be a necessity, it could be a luxury, it could be practical, or it could be for entertainment. These are all valid reasons, but you need to get clear about the value you are offering.

- **Who else sells it?** Someone else sells something similar. This is almost inevitable. You need to do background research into your competitors to see what they're doing and how you could do it better. Maybe they're doing really well. That doesn't mean you can't offer your own spin on a product, but you'll need to find your own voice and your own way of positioning it to stand out.

> **"Build something 100 people love, not something 1 million people kind of like."**
>
> **—BRIAN CHESKY (COFOUNDER AND CEO, AIRBNB)**

# WHY WE SELL: FOUR REASONS

This may seem obvious ("to make money, duh!"), or if you think about it too much, it may be more like a deep, philosophical question that leads you down the path of existential dread. Why do we do anything? Happily, we're not here for a philosophy lesson, so you can relax! But the basic question of why anyone sells anything is a fascinating one, and worth considering. Here are some of the reasons.

1. **To make a profit.** Obviously, we want what we sell to do well, to be popular, and to attract customers, so that we can make money and grow over time. The more customers we have, the more successful we are, and the more money we have. Hooray! As the business grows, we increase our reach ever farther to bring in more customers. It's an endless cycle, all leading to more satisfied buyers and ever-larger profits for us. At least, that's the hope. However, be mindful of the fact that this can't be all you want to get out of the arrangement. It's very easy to get profit-focused and ignore the human element. If you do that too often, you'll just alienate people and pretty soon you won't have many (or any) customers left.

2. **To bring value.** We have something useful, and we want the world (or at least a portion of it) to share in that value and improve their lives in some way. There is tremendous satisfaction in knowing that our product or service has helped others, improved their lives, or made them happy, and being able to see the results of that is indeed a lovely thing.

3. **To create and maintain new relationships.** Selling is about establishing trust and over time allowing that trust to develop into a good relationship, which may mean repeat customers, good word of mouth, and many other benefits. If someone is happy with what we offer, we want the chance to do it again for them at some point in the future.

4. **To change the world.** Well, maybe not right away, and honestly maybe not ever. But think about how many simple products have done just that over the past hundred years and more. Someone at some point thought to sell something that is now a household name and that we couldn't imagine being without. If that's your goal, it's a worthy one. Just be realistic about it. A lot of items and services on late-night infomercials were going to change everyone's lives at some point too, and they didn't. How much can what you sell make a real difference? That's the question you need to keep asking yourself.

> **"Sales is not about selling anymore, but about building trust and educating."**
>
> **—SIVA DEVAKI**

# WHY WE BUY: NINE REASONS

> **The psychology behind buying is, as you might expect, a complex subject. So much of what we buy every day is driven by wants, instead of needs. We all need food to survive, of course, but the food we actually buy is based on our tastes and preferences, rather than our physical needs. We could survive on a bowl of oatmeal, but we buy the burger instead because we prefer it.**

Many of the things that drive us to buy are unconscious—or at least we don't think all that much about them. Indeed, a lot of the reasons we buy anything may seem odd or even silly. Often when we read through lists like this, the reasons make us a little uncomfortable. A lot of readers will protest: "I don't do those things!" Actually, they probably do, and more often than you think. So, if you're ready, here are some of the real reasons people buy what they do.

1. **Safety:** Whether for psychological safety or physical safety, we buy to protect ourselves. If we already have basic necessities (food, clothing, shelter, and chocolate), we will often operate on the idea that having more things will make us even more safe (more chocolate actually does this; it's a scientific fact). Thus, having more clothes than we need, a bigger house, and more expensive food are all ways of convincing ourselves on some level that we're safer. Even with nonessentials, we are drawn to safety: a new car with extra safety features, a burglar alarm system, an online security system for our passwords, or a safe for valuables. These are legitimate concerns and needs, and they influence many of our buying decisions.

**2. Materialism as happiness:** More stuff makes us happy, right? Therefore, the more we have, the happier we will be. We're constantly told that accumulating lots of things won't make us feel better and that money doesn't buy happiness. And yet even if we go around saying these little reminders to ourselves and others,  we all secretly take some thrill in getting that new phone, that new pair of shoes, or that new expensive bottle of scotch. And there's nothing wrong with experiencing that thrill. But this often descends into an ongoing trap, where we *need* the latest phone, the faster car, the bigger house. Or we hoard, like dragons sleeping on their treasure. In the end, we find out that it doesn't make us that much happier, and maybe we learn the lesson, or maybe we don't. There's a saying to the effect that "the best things in life aren't things," and there's a lot of wisdom in those words.

**3. Competition:** This goes hand in hand with the idea of stuff making us happy. All too often we get caught up in what friends and peers are doing and buying, and fear of missing out (FOMO) takes over. Maybe we feel jealous because they just bought a new car or they're taking a nice vacation somewhere, and we want to keep up. Maybe we want them to see that we can do the same thing and are hoping to impress them by showing off what we have.

**4. Compensation:** We try to compensate for perceived deficiencies. We lack confidence, we have an emptiness to fill, or we seek admiration and approval from others. Material possessions temporarily make us feel better, but we usually find that before long, the feelings of inadequacy return and we want something else to fill the void.

5. **Selfishness:** Sometimes, people are just a bit greedy. Sorry to say, but we all are sometimes. Every now and then, we want something just because we want it. Impulse buys are a thing, and there can be a real thrill to accumulating new possessions as we grow our own personal little kingdoms. This can overlap with some of the other reasons listed above, of course.

## Wow, these all seem pretty awful! But there are also good reasons why we buy.

6. **For fun.** This is especially true when we buy tickets to an event, for example, or take a vacation. We're looking for adventure, for new experiences, for a good time. These are great reasons for wanting to spend our money, as research has shown that buying experiences brings us more long-term satisfaction (via great memories) than things do.

7. **For love.** We buy gifts for loved ones. We want to treat them to something special on their birthdays or at the holidays. Or maybe we buy gifts and make donations to charities we care about. Giving things gives us great satisfaction and is another worthy reason to buy.

8. **For our well-being.** We might sign up for a gym membership, or take a yoga class, or learn how to cook. We might buy a book on self-help or see a therapist. All of these kinds of efforts are made with the goal of improving ourselves, improving our health, or our mental state. This is less about selfishness and more about self-preservation.

9. **For education and growth.** If we invest in education or development, we're seeking to improve ourselves. This may be to give ourselves a boost career-wise by learning new information related to our jobs, but it might also be for personal benefit, such as learning a new

skill (cooking, woodworking, a language, etc.) or how to play a musical instrument. Maybe we want to go back to college and get that degree we never finished, or use that degree to change careers.

So, as you can see, the reasons we buy are varied and complex, some good and some bad, some selfish, some altruistic. And when we are selling, we should take into account all of these reasons and more. We'll never know exactly where a specific buyer is in their life at any given moment; all we can do is try to identify their need and fill it.

> ## "A goal is a dream with a deadline."
>
> **—NAPOLEON HILL**

# B2C AND B2B SALES

If you're in the business of selling, it's highly likely that you will focus on one of these two areas: Business to Consumer Sales and Business to Business Sales. You might even do both. They have some similarities, but also a good number of differences, so a brief definition of each is essential.

- **Business to Consumer (or Customer) Sales (B2C):** This is anything that goes out to the general public, from retail, to online, to a booth at a craft fair. You are selling products or services to people, everything from food to software to auto parts. If the customer is the end user of the product, it's a B2C sale; there's no middleman. This goes for services such as plumbing, housecleaning, or massage therapy. The customer directly benefits from what you sell and is the final destination for the product or service.

- **Business to Business Sales (B2B):** A large sector of sales is concerned with B2B selling. As the name implies, this involves selling what you produce to other businesses. These types of sales are usually more complex, bigger, more expensive, and take longer to complete. There are often several decision-makers along the way before the sale is finalized. But the market is vast and includes so many things that happen behind the scenes. A business may be selling a software solution to other companies; they may manufacture and sell equipment to hospitals; they may provide parts to an airline. These are a crucial part of the sales economy; they're just not the kind of transactions that the general public usually thinks about. When you're sitting on a jet waiting for takeoff, you're probably not wondering who sold the airline its intercom system.

It's sometimes said that B2C sales appeal to buyers' emotions, while B2B sales are more rational and designed to fill a specific need. If a hospital needs new beds, it buys them based on its budget and certain criteria, not on what makes the hospital buyer feel good, for example. And yet selling to either group still involves many of the same attitudes and strategies. If you are selling beds, you want the hospital representative to feel satisfied with the purchase, to trust you, to feel that they're not getting ripped off, and to be a repeat customer when the need comes up again. All of these things apply to whatever kind of sale you're making, and going in with the same ethical attitude to both B2C and B2B will benefit you in either case.

> **"Sales are contingent upon the attitude of the salesman, not the attitude of the prospect."**
>
> **—WILLIAM CLEMENT STONE**

# SOME IMPORTANT TYPES OF SALES

Beyond B2B and B2C, there are more detailed descriptions of sales types that you should know. In larger companies, these are sometimes done by different individuals or departments, but in a small business, you may be wearing several of these hats yourself.

- **Outside Sales:** As the name implies, outside sales is outwardly focused; it's not just someone who sells lawn furniture and gardening equipment! If it's B2B sales, the person doing the selling is very often out in the field: at other offices, meeting with prospective clients and customers, making presentations, on the phone, and so on. People that do this are outgoing, self-motivated, and like meeting other people. If that's not you, but you need this role in your business, then find someone who can do it for you!

- **Inside Sales:** This role involves maintaining and nurturing existing client relationships, your customers who are already on the inside. The person or persons handling this responsibility will be the go-to for clients who have questions, complaints, outrage, and other feedback. Again, this takes a certain kind of personality to do well, so remember that if you need this role for your business or if you're being asked to take it on. Recently, trends have been shifting away from outside sales to inside sales as one of the key ways a business attracts and keeps clients and customers, so this task is only going to get more important in the coming years.

- **Client Services:** Related to inside sales, client services provides, of course, services to clients. The person in this role may be the one that a customer is referred to by inside sales. The chief aim is keeping customers happy and on board. If you're doing your job and your product or service is all that you say it is,  this shouldn't be too difficult. But if you've been fudging things, promising what you can't deliver, or deceiving people to make the sale, you may have a much harder time of it. Bottom line: be ethical and do a good job. You'll keep your client-services person happy!

- **Lead Generation:** This is a form of marketing research and does pretty much what it sounds like it does: it looks around for potential new customers. And not just new customers, but the right ones, the ones who will enthusiastically buy what you're selling and come back for more. It also involves knowing when to let someone go, if it's not panning out the way you hoped it would.

- **Account Management:** As with client services, account management involves managing existing customers' accounts, but it also looks for ways that new business can be generated. One of the main tasks of an account manager is making sure that your existing clients stay that way and don't drift away to other sellers or services. What can you do to retain existing customers? What kinds of new products or innovations will you introduce to keep them interested and coming back? That heavy burden is on the back of the account manager, and it's absolutely essential to any business.

# YOU WON'T SELL TO EVERYONE, AND THAT'S OK

No matter how hard you try, no matter what you do, there will always be a large number of people who are just not interested in what you have to offer, or who waver between yes and no and then decide to walk away. Their reasons for doing so are pretty much infinite, and it's not something over which you have a lot of control. Even if they like what you're selling, they may be loyal to another brand, they may find a better deal elsewhere, or any number of other reasons why your specific product was not the one they chose to buy. This is fine, this is normal, and there's nothing you can do about it. Just accept that.

This is the main reason why you want to narrow your focus and target those that are in the niche(s) most receptive to what you are selling. Casting your net super wide and just assuming that you'll find your people is a big waste of time and money. Know who you're going after first and make the effort to reach out to those people. Unless your business is truly general (a grocery store, a pharmacy, etc.), it's unlikely that everyone will need what you're offering. Sure, big companies can afford to take out ads in major magazines and newspapers advertising to any and all who see them, but is this where you are right now? Probably not, so be careful and be focused. You wouldn't advertise your new steak restaurant in a vegetarian magazine (OK, you *might*, but it would be pretty foolish to do it!), so think about how what you're selling needs to be put in front of those most likely to buy it, and don't worry about the rest.

This is true even with the biggest of companies with products that seem to have universal appeal. Some people simply refuse to buy a PC, because they're loyal to Mac, or maybe they despise the iPhone and want another smartphone instead. They have a brand loyalty that they're very unlikely to switch from and trying to lure them away would be a waste of time.

Self-help teacher Rebecca Campbell puts it well; she's referring to one's personal life, but this just as easily can apply to business dealings: "You are not for everyone and that's OK. Talk to the people who can hear you. Don't waste your precious time and gifts trying to convince them of your value; they won't ever want what you're selling."

Being fine with the fact that you can't please all of the people all of the time is a great step forward and frees you from putting unnecessary pressure on yourself.

[
## "Don't celebrate closing a sale, celebrate opening a relationship."

### —PATRICIA FRIPP
]

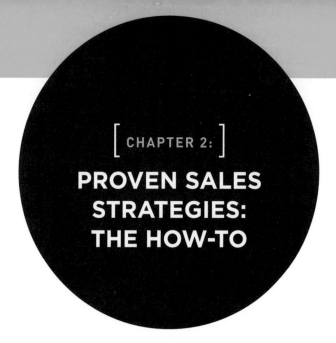

# CHAPTER 2

# PROVEN SALES STRATEGIES: THE HOW-TO

Selling is an art, selling is a science, and selling is everything in between! There is no one way to do it; it will be unique to each individual, customer, business, and selling situation. That being said, there are some time-honored practices that will help you wade through the potential minefield of sales booby traps and pitfalls. Once you learn the following techniques, you'll be well on your way to understanding the process and even understanding your own sales needs and goals much better. Selling is a specific practice, and you have to get specific about how you go about it. The more prepared you are, the better.

# WHAT IS PROSPECTING?

Prospecting is the first thing you'll do in a sales situation. It's the process of reaching out by various methods to start generating leads, including phone calls, emails, research, networking, face-to-face discussions, chasing down former leads that have gone cold, and much more. Like prospectors for gold, you're looking for those little nuggets among the dirt and runoff that will yield great things. As you turn up more and more leads and reach out across your targeted areas, you'll find that you have two basic categories, possibilities and prospects, out of which a third, customer, can come.

- **Possibilities:** These are people or businesses in your targeted demographics that may be interested in what you offer, but they don't yet know about you, or they haven't heard enough. You'll need to reach out to them (via advertising, cold calling, or whatever method is best) to see if they might become eventual customers. If they might, then they can become prospects.

- **Prospects:** These are the individuals or companies with whom you've made some contact and who might be interested in buying from you at some point. A prospect is one who has not yet bought from you but has at least shown some interest. A prospect remains a prospect during the entire sales process, but once they buy, that all changes.

- **Customers:** Customers are prospects that have bought from you, now or at some point in the past. The goal is to make sure that they are satisfied with their purchase and to keep them engaged in your ongoing business, so they turn into repeat customers. Repeat customers are the true prize  of prospecting, the gold nuggets when all else has washed away. When people or businesses return to you over and over because they're satisfied with what you sell and they feel a loyalty to your brand, you have something beautiful and valuable. Guard it well and take care of it!

[

**"The definition of salesmanship is the gentle art of letting the customer have it your way."**

**—RAY KROC**

]

# WHO IS IN YOUR TARGET AUDIENCE? FIVE WAYS TO IDENTITY IT

As we've said so far, your audience will not be everyone out there with a brain and some money to spend, much as you'd like it to be. The more you can be specific about the kinds of customers you want to attract, the better. Here is a list of considerations and actions to take as you're putting your plan for world domination (also known as increased sales) together.

1. **Do your research.** This is obvious, but it's going to take some digging in to really find out about your people, who they are, what they want, and where they are. The same goes if you're selling to other businesses. The Resources section has some websites and online tools that will be helpful with your initial research.

2. **Narrow it down.** You need to be very focused. If you're selling to customers, you need to figure out whom your product appeals to. Ask yourself questions about the age range, economic status, location, education levels, interests and tastes, and anything else you think is relevant to what you sell. If you're selling to other companies, think about their location and reach, their size and economic strength, and perhaps most basic of all, is it a business that needs what you're selling? Don't waste time on businesses outside of your parameters, whether it's that they're too far away, not close enough in industry to match your ideal customer, not big enough, or whatever other criteria you set.

3. **Do your values align?** Is the company you want to sell to doing things that you approve of? Is there something about them that bothers you, such as the way they treat their employees or how they behave in the community? Is their rep off-putting when talking to you? This is all important information to consider when looking at developing a long-term sales relationship with another business. If you're selling to people, are there some demographics to whom you'd rather not sell? We're not talking about discrimination here; it's more a sense of what you stand for as a company and how you want your products to be received and advertised.

4. **Imagine your ideal customer.** Who is the perfect customer for you? Let your mind be free to range over the possibilities and see what comes up. This is not indulging in wishful thinking; it's actually a very helpful exercise to narrow down the types of people you want to do business with. The clearer you can be with that in your mind, the more you'll be likely to go looking for just those kinds of customers. Is there just one industry or section of the public that you want to serve? That's fine; it can help you get clear about who will be your best prospects.

5. **Refine your marketing.** Now that you have some ideas about who is the best fit, you'll need to tailor your marketing to those audiences. Marketing is a vast topic in and of itself, and beyond the scope of this book. For help, see *This Book Will Teach You Marketing Fundamentals*—also in the same series. The idea is to target those specific groups with messages that they will want to hear and respond to.

# BUILDING A DATABASE OF POTENTIAL CUSTOMERS AND EXISTING ONES

Building a database for your potential and actual customers is a great idea, and will likely save you a lot of work later on. Databases are useful both if you are seeking potential new business customers (they're great for adding contact and other relevant information), and if you have existing customers (whether those customers are other businesses or the general public, databases are essential for keeping in touch). Here are the steps to take to get started.

- **Acquire suitable database software.** Again, this seems obvious, but you'll need a suitable program to work with. Make sure that you can import and export materials from other programs easily, as you'll probably be doing a lot of that! Customer relationship management (CRM) software such as HubSpot Sales, Pipedrive, EngageBay, Freshsales, and others can make your life much easier!

- **Decide what information you'll need to store.** For businesses, this may be the company name and address, your key point of contact and their information (phone, email, etc.), and maybe other information, such as if they are a prospect or an ongoing client and details about previous contracts. When requesting that users fill out the sign-up form, keep it clear and brief, and don't ask for more information than you need. For a customer in the general public, their name and email address (and maybe a phone number) should be enough. Anything much beyond that may seem intrusive; you don't want to be seen as stalking your customers or data mining them! Commit to assuring them that you won't share their data with others beyond what the law requires and that you will not spam them, and stick to this!

- **When gathering information from the general public, always ask permission!** If you are compiling a customer mailing list (whether business or general public), always make sure that the sign-up option is just that: optional. You also always have to give them a chance to opt out at any time. All good mailing list programs such as Mailchimp and Constant Contact automatically take care of this.

- **Determine what your database will be used for.** Again, this may seem obvious, but you may find that you need more than one for different reasons. Databases can be great for several reasons:

  - **They can be used for marketing and prospecting.** Obviously, having a list of all your current and potential customers gives you a great opportunity to reach out when you have something new and exciting to sell them! You can make these campaigns very personalized and based on criteria that you have in the database, so that if one of your products isn't for everyone on your list, you don't have to annoy them with ads for it.

  - **They can be used for analysis of purchases.** Keeping track of who buys what is a great way to see what's selling and how your advertising is working. It gives you useful feedback that lets you modify your strategies as you go. Keep the good and eject the bad! Depending on how much a customer opts in to sharing data with you, you may be able to analyze some of their other spending habits and site visits to see how your products may best serve them.

- **They can predict future purchases.** You may be able to use data about purchasing to get a sense of what customers will buy from you again and when.

• **Organize the fields in your database to be useful.** Make everything clear and consistent from entry to entry. You don't want to be searching for information for a potential important client because it's not stored in the same way as the other entries. Take the time to input each one correctly, and you'll thank yourself later. This will help prevent annoying mistakes, such as duplicate entries; sometimes people have more than one email address, for example. Make sure that your information is organized in a way to prevent these kinds of embarrassing mistakes.

• **Decide early on who can access what.** You may have several people working at your company who will need to work with the database for different reasons. Determine who is authorized to access what information and for what purposes. There will be logins and passwords for this, so get that sorted out at the beginning.

> **"You have to generate revenue as efficiently as possible. And to do that, you must create a data-driven sales culture. Data trumps intuition."**
>
> **—DAVE ELKINGTON**

# NINE TIPS FOR MAPPING OUT YOUR SALES PLAN

A sales plan is different from a business plan in that its aim is to improve and increase your sales, rather than defining the company's overall goals. Your plan needs to take into consideration all of the information you've gathered so far and use it to assemble a coherent sales strategy that will yield great results. Sure, no problem! To be honest, it isn't that difficult; it just takes some preparation. Here are some tips for how to go about it.

1. **Define your mission.** Go back to your overall business plan and remind yourself of who you are and why you're doing what you're doing. It's good to revisit this, as it will give you a clearer sense of what you want to bring to the table.

2. **Be mindful of your brand.** Your brand is your total identity, your reputation that grows over time with each new satisfied customer. You want to be sure that your next sales campaign is in line with what you've already established. For further information on brand creation, see *This Book Will Teach You Marketing Fundamentals*—also in this series.

3. **Define who's with you.** If you have a team, it's a good idea to figure out who is doing what right at the beginning of the process. Maybe your company is large enough to have a dedicated sales team, but it's just as possible that you work for a smaller business where everyone is pitching in a little to do everything.

4. **Review your target market(s).** Again, who are you going to be selling to? Are you sure you've found the right demographics or businesses? Clarify everything before you launch into your work. If you get a few months into your plan and find that a given market isn't feasible, you'll have wasted valuable time and money.

5. **Set realistic goals.** Take into consideration month-to-month and end-of-the-year results. What do you want to achieve sales-wise? How can you do it? Is it even possible to do it (that goes with the being realistic part)? What are the upcoming trends? Consider things such as the size of your market, the position you're currently in, how well you've done so far, and how well the people in charge of your sales will be able to do their job. Goals can be revenue-based (wanting to make a certain amount of money by a certain time) or volume-based (wanting to attract a specific new set of customers or complete a certain number of sales in a given time period). Either or both is fine, but, again, they need to be clear and realistic.

6. **Make sure that your plan is well mapped-out with specific completion dates and milestones set down.** If you have a yearlong plan in front of you, you need to be able to track your progress week by week, month by month, and so on. If you have specific targets that you set for yourself to be done in two weeks' time, you have a much better chance of achieving them if you have them set in stone and you force yourself to keep on track.

7. **Who are you competing with?** You will undoubtedly have others selling similar products and services. What will they be doing in the same coming period? Define your similarities and differences, and see if they're doing something better than you are. They probably are, but you're probably doing something better than they are, too!

8. **What will you be offering?** In this sales period, are you offering any special promotions or discounts? Are there other ways you want to try to lure in new prospects and increase awareness of what you sell? How will you implement these strategies? Compare these ideas to the calendar and deadlines you've set for yourself.

9. **What is your budget during this calendar period?** What can you afford for marketing, advertising, employee pay, and so on? You will ideally be spending money to make money, so be sure that you keep a close watch on your businesses finances and don't go over budget.

> [ **"Stop saying 'later.' You WON'T do it later. Do it or decide not to do it."**
> —*CHRIS BROGAN* ]

# START WITH YOUR NETWORK: PROFESSIONAL AND PERSONAL

When you want to reach new people and businesses, it's always great to start with whom you know. This is true for networking, marketing, and especially for sales. Instead of starting cold, you have a chance to reach out to others via mutual connections, which can give you a head start on selling and promoting. This approach is especially useful if you are a new business that doesn't have a big reputation yet. What better way to get known than by trusted recommendations from your family, friends, and business colleagues? Here are some ways you can leverage this built-in help to your advantage.

- **Reach out to family and friends and let them know about what you're doing, but be careful.** If you have family or friends with business connections, it's well worth putting a word in their ears to let them know all about your sales plans. Bear in mind that if you are not close or have lost touch, it might seem a bit weird to just contact them out of the blue offering your sales pitch. Just as with any other relationship, you need to cultivate a good feeling of interaction and trust. If you've lost touch with friends or family members over time, contact them first and catch up before moving on to any business talk. Ask yourself how you would feel if you were in their situation. Commit to keeping in touch. Remember that if they're not the kind of people whom you are interested in hanging out with, they are probably not the kind of people you can sell to or who will help you with your sales goals.

- **Business contacts can be helpful, but again be careful.** It's possible that you have many colleagues and business connections that could be of use, but just as with your family and personal friends, reach out to them with care. Out-of-the-blue greetings asking for help or information will seem odd and imposing. Have a genuine reason for reestablishing contact before diving into your sales jargon. Be careful about office politics as well, if you are contacting people from a previous workplace. Be sure that you left without any controversy or bad feelings, and that you're not asking them to do something that would violate their own code of conduct, share proprietary information, or engage in any other unethical or illegal activity.

- **Be genuine about what you do and what you love, and others will see that.** People very often can smell a phony a kilometer away. If you're not committed to your work and are only trying to use it to make some quick cash, you're going to come across as insincere, and the people who know you best will probably see right through it. On the other hand, if you're following a dream or a passion, you're working hard at it, you know it inside and out, and improving your sales is an important part of realizing your goals, you'll be seen as much more sincere and trustworthy, because you are.

- **Be wary of biases.** Because they are your friends and family, or work colleagues, they may not be the best judge of your plans, if you're seeking feedback. They want you to succeed and may not be able to provide valuable constructive criticism, or they may not offer it out of fear of offending you. Sometimes, it really is better to seek out a stranger's advice, rather than someone who could inadvertently hurt your chances out of a genuine desire for you to succeed. A cold call could be a much better gauge of how your selling plan is working than a friendly conversation with your sibling or cousin.

# SEVEN WAYS TO OVERCOME THE FEAR OF REACHING OUT

Making contact with new potential clients and customers is absolutely essential to the business of selling, but it also comes with a lot of anxiety. For many, it's almost like stage fright. You're in the spotlight, others are looking at you, you may mess up, others might ridicule you, the earth may open up and swallow you while you're trying (to be fair, that last one almost never happens). Anxieties about putting ourselves out there are very real and very valid, so don't let anyone tell you otherwise. We each bring our own personal backgrounds and issues to the table, but there are some ways to make the experience less stressful. If you find that you have a genuine anxiety or phobia about some aspect of putting yourself out there, please seek some professional guidance or help. These kinds of fears can be overcome, and in the long run you'll be glad you made the effort to do so.

1. **Set simple goals that you know you can achieve.** Don't resolve to call a hundred people this week if the idea of even calling one makes you tremble. Focus on that one first. If all you can do is make three calls by Friday, set that as your target and stick to it. You may find that those calls go better than you feared, and then you'll be ready to do more. If that's the case, go for it!

2. **Remind yourself of the value you have and the value you bring.** You're not some unworthy annoyance who's wasting other

people's time. You bring something of real value to others, something that they want and need, and now you're reaching out to them. Remind yourself of your experience and accomplishments. Write these down and refer to them often. Keep a list beside you while you're calling. Write down all the things you know will benefit those who buy from you.

3. **Focus on the experience being about your potential customer, not you.** It isn't about how well you present yourself. It's about offering something special that can help others. When you take the focus off you, the pressure goes down a little.

4. **Be realistic about your results.** The first few (or first many) calls may not go well; you may get nothing from them. But use each as a learning tool to refine and get better. Every time you do it, you're practicing, and with each practice, you'll improve a little, just like playing the piano or learning to drive a car. Remember the first time you ever sat behind the wheel of a car, ready to be taught how to drive? That was pretty nerve-racking. But you got the hang of it and now you probably think nothing of it. The process *will* get easier over time, honest.

5. **Be well-prepared in each instance.** Have a script, practice it, memorize it, run it past your friends and colleagues, but tailor it to each unique new contact. The less you feel like you're making things up as you go along, the more relaxed you will be.

6. **Remember that most other people feel the same.** Very few people are naturals at sales or reaching out, and it's always awkward the first time or the first hundred times. Remind yourself that you're doing something special that a lot of people may not even have the courage to try—at least you're giving it a go!

7. **If you do get a good result, celebrate it!** It's a sign that you're doing the right thing. Be proud of yourself, buy that piece of chocolate cake (or whatever appeals to you), and then get right back to it!

# DON'T BE PUSHY: EIGHT WAYS OF INTRODUCING YOURSELF WITHOUT SELLING SOMETHING

Yes, you want to sell what you have. No, you don't want to look like a salesperson. How often have you met someone making the hard sell to you, even if it was just in a store? It's pretty annoying and puts you off very quickly. A lot of people don't even like being asked if they need help when they're in a retail situation. To be fair, a lot of store employees are required to do this, so it's not really their fault. But it always runs the risk of turning off a possible customer; some people really just want to browse by themselves in peace. Still, you have to be able to make your case, create a sense of urgency (see pages 58–59), and gently nudge someone toward a yes. So how to you find the balance? These pieces of advice work whether you're running a shop or cold calling reps at multinational corporations. In the end, it's all about courtesy.

1. **Don't pressure them.** Creating a sense of need for a product is fine, but pressuring the buyer is not. If they feel threatened or bullied, they'll walk away.

**2. Don't pressure yourself.** Acting as if every
sale is crucial to your survival is not a great way
to go about things. You won't make every sale,
you just won't. Treating each potential customer
as important is essential, but don't start each
transaction from a position of fear that if you
don't grab them, all is lost. Scarcity mindsets
don't work. You're better off using each sale as a

learning tool, to refine and make your pitch better as you go. There will
always be more customers out there, and you'll never stop looking for
new ones.

**3. Don't start with the sales pitch.** When
you are approaching someone on the phone or in
an email, make it about them. Then make it about
their needs. Then offer up a potential solution,
if they'd like to have further discussions about it.
If you start with "Hi! I have exactly what you're
looking for!" you're just going to get hung up on
or ignored.

**4. Invite the prospect to do the talking.** If they seem interested
in you, it's good to let them lead the conversation. Ask many questions
and gather information. Your concern should be for them, not for making
a quick sale. Once you know what their specific needs are, you'll be in a
better position to offer a good solution.

**5. Don't shut down their objections.** If there's something that's
not sitting right with them, don't belittle it or dismiss it. And don't counter
with "but" as if it's not a real concern. The goal is to listen and take in
everything. Whatever the problem is, they have a legitimate reason for
bringing it up, so take it seriously.

6. **Don't insist that they need to do something or should do it.** It can come off as a bit overbearing, even bullying. They know their business or life better than you (despite your research), so telling them that they're doing something wrong will be a big turnoff. Even if you mean your suggestion kindly, it's not a great strategy. Never be seen as telling them what to do.

7. **Don't keep them on the hook longer than necessary.** If you're having a phone conversation or an in-person meeting, respect their time and don't try to keep them around past the few minutes you've agreed to speak or the fifteen minutes of your in-person meeting. Offer to have a follow-up call or meeting if things are going well. Unless, of course, your prospect wants to talk more and asks if you can stick around, in which case, by all means go for it!

8. **Take no for an answer.** Yes, this one is hard, but sometimes (often) what you're offering is not for them. It's fine to ask if you can check in again in three months or six months, or whatever, but when they just don't want or need it now (or ever), be gracious, accept it, and thank them for their time. If you badger them, whine, or push them with a hard sell, you're pretty much guaranteed to never have them as a customer in the future. And you'll get a bad reputation, because word about things like that spreads. Oh yes, it does!

# THE COLD CALL

Cold calling is one of those activities that fills almost everyone with dread. The idea of picking up the phone (or touching the screen, as the case may be) and randomly reaching out to people whom you don't know and who may have no interest in what you have to say is terrifying. It's almost as bad as public speaking. Our minds are instantly flooded with fear, our hearts race, and our hands shake. Can't we do something else instead? Who needs a phone anyway? We can just send them a postcard! Well, like it or not, the world still runs on phone calls, and using your phone as an actual phone once in a while is something you'll probably have to get used to. But it's not all that bad. No, really. Here are some tips for getting the most out of reaching out in initial calls, and taking some of the fear out while doing it!

- **First of all, it's *not* random calling.** You're not just dialing people at random and seeing what happens. You *could* do that, of course, but it will just waste your time and stress you out. Cold calling involves a lot of preparation and research. Once again, you have narrowed down your list to only those contacts that are most likely to be receptive your message. If you've found the exact person you need to contact, great! But sometimes you'll have to go through gatekeepers, even if it's just a receptionist.

- **Research how many calls you need to make and what is the best time to make them.** What is your cold-calling target for the week or month? Draw up a list and stick to it. Research the best time to make your calls. It may vary from business to business, but afternoons from Tuesdays to Thursdays are often considered the best times. On Mondays, everyone is overwhelmed by the week's tasks and may have numerous calls and emails already to deal with. Friday is . . . well, Friday. If someone called you at 4:30 p.m. on a Friday afternoon trying to sell something, would you *really* want to listen?

- **Have a script ready.** We cannot stress this enough: have a script ready! Never just wing it and see what happens. Obviously, you want to tailor your words to this particular client, but it's absolutely essential to have something to refer to. Practice it over and over until you are comfortable with it. Have someone else listen to you and give you feedback. In fact, it's great to have someone pretend to be a potential customer and have them react accordingly. Let them raise objections so that you can practice getting around those. Commit much of it to memory if you can, but you'll also need to keep it at hand for the real call.

- **You may not reach the person right away.** If you get someone else answering first, ask to be transferred to your target. You may well be asked what this is regarding, so be honest and explain your purpose, without going into detailed explanations. Often, they just want to know you're calling the right place.

- **You may get their voice mail.** If you get through, great; but you may get sent to your target's voice mail. It happens all the time. Leave a brief message of thirty seconds or less, about who you are and the purpose of your call (remember, you're not selling anything yet!), and offer to call back later. Always follow up on this promise. They may return your call, in which case, great! It means that they at least want to hear what you have to say. But you may be in the position of having to call back. Wait an appropriate amount of time; it may be later that day, it may be the following day, but just make sure that you try again.

- **Or you may actually get through to them (gulp!).** OK, they've answered the phone and now your nervousness can really kick into high gear! What do you do? Help! First, remember that you're there to start a conversation, not sell them something. You are *speaking with* them, not *talking to* them. So, instead, say something like: "Hi, this is XXXX from [your business]. I'm impressed with [whatever they do], and am phoning to see if [what we offer, do] can help to improve [whatever their need is] and benefit your team. Do you have two minutes?" Keep the conversation focused on them, not you.

- **If they say yes to speaking with you.** Great! Give a very brief overview of what you can do for them, and perhaps try set up a time when you can speak in more detail.

- **If they say no to speaking with you.** It might not be a good time for them for any number of reasons. Respect that and don't try to keep them on the phone. Try to reschedule at a time more convenient to them. If they agree, then great! You've moved the conversation one step further. But what if they're just not interested?

- **If they say, "No thank you."** If this happens (and it will), they've probably rejected you and your amazing offer. There are many techniques for overcoming initial objections, and it's worth taking the time to learn some of them, but you ultimately may be faced with the awful fact that they're just not interested or just don't need what you're offering, at least right now. Accept that and thank them for their time. But this door might not be closed forever. It may be that in six months, their situation will have changed. Never give up entirely unless they tell you something definitive, such as all of that work is done in-house or they have a five-year contract with someone else already in place.

- **Accept that you will be rejected a lot.** Yes, this is the tough part. It's entirely possible that most of your calls will result in a "no thank you," and it's hard not to take it personally. But remember, it's very, very likely not to be personal, unless you've said something offensive or just plain dumb, and you know you're not doing that, right? Dealing with rejection is hard in any area of our lives, so don't feel bad about feeling bad. Some suggest that you can turn it around by having a little contest with yourself or coworkers: What's the weirdest/worst/funniest rejection you received this week? Inject a little fun into the process, and you may find that the sting goes away more quickly! Also, use rejections to fine-tune your message, and see what works and what doesn't.

> **"Most of the important things in the world have been accomplished by people who have kept on trying when there seemed to be no hope at all."**
>
> **—DALE CARNEGIE**

# THE COLD EMAIL AND THE WARM EMAIL

Email can be a very useful tool for reaching out to potential clients and customers, and this is great news for all of you phone-phobes! Of course, it's important to try out multiple methods of contact and see which methods work best for you, but email can yield very good results, if done right.

- **Cold emailing:** This is similar to cold calling, but obviously the difference is that the first contact is made by email. The benefits are that these can be less intrusive, more relaxed, and for you, the sender, far less stressful. You can write and rewrite your message until you get it exactly the way you want it. The downside is that emails don't have the immediacy of a phone conversation, and your message may get caught in a spam filter or otherwise never be seen by the intended recipient. And if they receive large amounts of email, they may ignore it anyway.

- **The warm email:** This is a term sometimes used to stress how to make your emails more personal. As with calling, you need to narrow your focus, find the exact person you need to contact, and personalize your message.

- **Have a good subject line.** This is the first (and maybe) only thing they will see, so you have to catch their attention. Keep it client-focused: "We love the work you're doing with XXXX" or "Congratulations on meeting XXXX goal!" Be personalized, be creative, but don't be silly or boring!

- **Personalize it and make it about them.** You must give a personal greeting (*never* something like "Dear Sir/Madam") and lead with the addressee. Don't just launch into what you do or offer; that will almost guarantee an instant deletion! If you've researched your prospect, try leading with something about them. Did they win an award or pass an important milestone that was in the news recently? Congratulate them about it. Do you admire something they've done? Let them know!

- **Briefly explain the purpose of your email.** It's OK at this point to talk about why you're contacting them, but again, make it about solving a problem they have. Always be client-oriented.

    - **Include a call to action.** Ask if you can chat on the phone briefly, when they have time. Always make it convenient for them.

- **Thank them for their time and include your sign off.** That's it. That's all you need to do. That wasn't so scary, was it? Just make sure to include all of your contact information in your email signature, so that if they're very interested, they can get back to you. You might even get a surprise phone call!

- **Wait and see what happens.** They may respond quickly, they may take a few days, or they may not respond at all. Any and all of these scenarios will happen. Just remember that if they don't get back to you right away, that's not necessarily an indication that they're not interested. People get busy, things get filed away, emails get lost. Wait a certain number of days (anything from three days to a week) and then send a follow-up email if you haven't heard back. This is normal and perfectly acceptable. Then, you have to wait again. And again, you may not hear back. Some prospectors will tell you that you have to try three to five times to get a response, and this may seem exasperating, but it's good advice to keep in mind.

- **What if they never respond?** It will happen a lot. Some people are just not interested. You may have sent four emails and waited three weeks, and heard nothing back. At this point, you'll need to decide if this potential client or customer is someone you really need to go after. They could be sending you the message that they are not interested, without actually having to tell you. Or they may just be really busy and keep meaning to get back to you at some point. If the email hasn't brought you any results, you may consider switching over to a follow-up phone call, which can give you a definitive answer on whether they're interested or not.

> **"We need to stop interrupting what people are interested in and be what people are interested in."**
>
> **—CRAIG DAVIS**

# NEVER, EVER SPAM!

Spam is evil; we all hate it, so don't do it. When you're trying to sell, you should never be throwing everything at the wall to see what sticks; you're trying to narrow the scope down to your best possible customers and keep the ones you already have. Blitzing a million emails out to everyone in your city is going to get you nowhere and will earn you a bad reputation quickly. We all know not to do these kinds of spammy things, but here are few important points to keep in mind about mailing lists and the etiquette of contacting others.

- **For goodness' sake, never buy a list of emails!**
This is a sleazy old tactic that goes all the way back to the 1990s, and is a virtual guarantee that you'll be blocked and reported. Either the people on them didn't sign up for them, the email addresses no longer exist, or any emails you send are forwarded to shady addresses that will then add *you* to their spam lists. Every single contact on your mailing lists needs to be a real person who is there because they signed up for it and has a way to opt out at any time. No exceptions.

- **Don't contact people too often.** If you make a habit of sending out too much communication, people will tire of it. Have you ever signed up on an email list only to find that the company starts sending you ads and promotions literally every day? How long did that last? You probably unsubscribed by day four, so keep that in mind when it's your turn to send out stuff. People on your list don't need to hear from you every day, unless you have specifically said that they will receive a daily post about something (think of Seth Godin, for example, who posts short business insights every day). Even better, offer multiple options so that they can opt in to what they want to receive. Some may only want your monthly newsletter, while others may want weekly tips. Allow people to customize what they receive from you, and they'll thank you for it!

- **Be mindful of your content to avoid being reported.** Gmail, Yahoo Mail, and many other programs use spam reports to create a "sender score" about your IP. If your emails get reported too often in a given time period, these services will start flagging your emails as spam, and they'll go immediately into your contacts' spam folders. Yeah, you don't want this to happen, because once you get locked in that jail cell, it's a lot more difficult to get out than it was to get in. The recipient has to take the time to mark your email as "not spam," and how many will honestly bother to do that?

- **Certain key words and symbols can also trigger spam filters if they're overused.** Words like "money" and "free," along with using all-capitalized words ("AMAZING") or too many exclamation points ("Check it out!!!!") can all be warning signs that will cause your precious message to be relegated to a spam filter. Look at some of the spam you've received and see what's in it. Try to avoid any obvious red flags.

- **Use a mail program.** Constant Contact, Mailchimp, iContact, and various others have all the tools put in place to send out large amounts of emails and to let you design and customize them as you like. Their analytics let you see how many emails were opened so that you can gauge response rate. They'll even let you do an A/B trial, so that you can try out two different forms of a message and see which one gets a better response.

Also, they will let you know if an email address is no longer valid so you can remove it from your list (some studies show that up to 30 percent of emails are changed or go dead every year!). Most of these services are free up to a certain number of users or monthly mailings, and then charge fees over that, but this is an investment that your business needs, and it will save you a lot of potential problems and headaches later on!

[
## "Every email is an opportunity to test a different benefit or angle."

*—HEATHER MORGAN*
]

# SIX WAYS TO CREATE URGENCY

Urgency doesn't mean making things urgent or worrying for your potential customer. In fact, that's the last thing you want to do! It's about creating an environment where this person or business doesn't want to put things off for a few days or a week before making their decision to buy. Rather, they feel that they will benefit more if the sale goes through now. There are many ways to create urgency, and these are some of the most common.

1. **Make sure that they really want the product or service.** If you don't establish this right from the beginning, it's not likely that dangling carrots and discounts are going to make them change their minds. You should have found the right target or demographic if you've done your marketing and selling research carefully. That they want what you're selling should be a given, not a hope.

2. **Create deadlines.** Often, we want to put a customer at ease by assuring them that there's no obligation to buy. We don't want to come across as the smarmy used-car salesman desperate for a sale. At the same time, relieving them of any obligations makes it much more likely that they'll walk away. Limited-time offers exist for a reason. And don't let your deadlines be too far in the future. If you're selling products, especially to the general public, offering a discount until 5:00 p.m. on Thursday is a great way of making something more urgent, if the customer sees the ad on Tuesday. They can think about it, but they have to make up their minds within a window of time, or they'll miss out. And on that note . . .

3. **Play up fear of missing out (FOMO).** Deadlines, a limited supply in stock (be specific about how many), a service that will only be a one-time offer before rates go up: these not only create urgency, but also they amplify the fear of missing out. If your customers know that they might not get in on a great deal, it may motivate them to decide to purchase sooner rather than later.

4. **Make the process as easy as possible.** If you are selling something that requires paperwork, extra fees, and so on, offer to help out with those or waive the fees. Auto dealerships do this kind of thing all the time, especially at the holidays. The buyer can avoid the taxes and fees (paid for by the dealer) or get money back at signing. It's designed to get people in the doors looking for a great and hassle-free deal.

5. **Offer bonuses and incentives.** As in the car-dealership example above, you can advertise not only what they won't get if they don't make a decision but also what they *will* get if they do. In fact, this kind of motivation can be stronger than a negative one. "Order by Friday at midnight, and we'll throw in at no extra charge . . ." Just make sure that what you're offering has genuine value and is something they'd rather have than not have. Make it count!

6. **Remind them of what they want or need.** If you can, it's great to keep this in their minds during the whole process. You can explain the benefits that their purchase will bring them or mention the problem that they need to be solved. It will forge a link between what they need and what you're offering.

# PROBLEM-AGITATE-SOLUTION

> This is a well-known copywriter's technique for creating advertising copy that will motivate readers to take action on buying what they want and need. It's a way of gently getting into their heads and convincing them that now is the time to take action on that item or service that they've been thinking about getting.

- **Problem:** You need to understand what the problem is, so that you can analyze it and then amplify it in your communications. The point is to vividly highlight the problem, so that readers will connect and consider taking action. You'll need to know your product or service inside and out so that you can be in a position to step up and offer your solution. If you're not sure, find out first. Be sure that you communicate the problem in language that your target demographic understands.

- **Agitate:** Now you want to bring the problem to life for your potential customer. If someone says, "Oh, man, this happens to me all the time! I really wish I could figure out how to fix it. Hmmm, this ad is interesting," you're well on your way to winning them over. You want to describe how the problem will only get worse if nothing is done about it by using examples, real-life stories, or similar techniques to reinforce that the issue is real and needs to be dealt with. The trick, of course, is not to overdo it. You want potential customers to be agitated just enough that they decide to take action. You don't want them to be overwhelmed and run away in despair! Most importantly, you want them to feel that you empathize with them, because you do, and if you don't, you should. Customers are your lifeblood, and you need to treat them well and be on their side.

- **Solution:** Happily for your customers, you're here to save the day, hooray! Well, that's how you want them to feel. And happily, you really *do* have the solution to their problem. Show them what you have and how it works. Prove to them via testimonials that you are worthy of their trust. Offer a significant call to action that they can take right now that will get them on the way to having that solution in their lives.

## Here's how it might all look in a hypothetical ad:

"Concerned about a tough laundry stain? Worried that your favorite shirt or trousers might be ruined forever because of one unfortunate accident? Don't despair! XXXX has been clinically proven to remove the toughest stains in just one wash. Oil, paint, wine, blood: all of these are no match for XXXX! Order now and get a free travel bottle with your purchase."

How many ads have you seen with similar wording? Probably most of them. Variations on this template are a standard kind of ad copy that still works, and they still get results. Make use of it!

> # "The best marketing doesn't feel like marketing."
>
> **—TOM FISHBURNE**

# FREE SAMPLES AND TRIALS

> Another great way to lure in potential customers and clients is by offering a freebie up front. You're saying that you want them to try your product with no obligation, take it for a test run, and see if it's a good fit. Obviously, this works better with some products than others. If you own a restaurant, offering a coupon for a free starter or side is a great way to invite new customers in to try your menu. They're getting something (food) for free, and you have the chance to show off your amazing menu to people who might not otherwise have stepped through the door. Grocery stores often have free samples available, because they want you to buy a new product on their shelves. If you like it and put it in your basket, that's an instant sale.

Software companies do this kind of promotion often. They'll offer a free trial version of the program (sometimes with some advanced functions disabled) that may be good for a week or a month. You're free to try it out, get to know it, and see how it works. At the end of that time, you can upgrade to the full version and buy it, or you're free to move on and try other things. Some will even let you keep using the free version, but offer additional features for a version that you purchase to subscribe to (known as upselling, see page 118). There are endless ways to make this kind of offer work. Here are some things to keep in mind.

- **Make sure that the free offering actually has value.**
  Whether it's food or a free trial, the potential customer has to feel like they've gotten something of value from the experience. Don't skimp on this. If you're offering a trial of your software, make sure it's actually something a customer can use. You'll still see some free software that will

let you play around with it, but won't, for example, let you save your photo, audio file, or written work. Seriously, what is the point of that?! You want them to come away with a good experience, so let them take something from it. If they like it, they'll upgrade. If you're offering a free starter at your restaurant, don't just give them a glass full of breadsticks. Make it something memorable that they would want to pay money for on a repeat visit. Always offer genuine value.

- **Make sure they know how to purchase the product or service, if/when they want.** This should seem obvious, but you want to make the experience as enjoyable and easy for the customer as possible. If they like what they get, you may just get an instant sale! If you are a physical store, then obviously they know where to come back when they want to buy, but online, it's important to have buttons with links always visible. Free software, for example, should always have an upgrade option visible. Just don't make it obnoxious!

- **Make sure they know how to use the product.** If it requires any kind of instruction, it's crucial that you make this freely available to your customers. If you're offering a trial of some new program for a business, you may even want to send someone over to demonstrate how to use it. This is a great way to highlight its many functions and get more people on board.

- **This is a great strategy for services, too.** Think about how many professionals, such as lawyers, offer a free half-hour consultation. Not everyone who comes in will hire them, but it gives the two parties a chance to get to know each other, the lawyer an opportunity to decide if the case has merit, and the potential client a chance to state their case in a pressure-free environment. Two-for-one coupons work very well with this kind of model, too. A dry cleaner may offer to clean a second garment for free when the customer has the first one cleaned. These are great ways to promote the business and bring in new customers. The incentive of the freebie is a powerful one and should never be ignored if you can work it into your selling strategy.

# CONTINUING THE DIALOGUE AFTER THE SALE

You've made a sale! Awesome! But as you probably know, your work is really only beginning. Depending on the nature of your product or service, you may want to keep this customer over a period of time, and with luck, sell to them again down the line. Here are some things you should do to make sure that you'll have not only a satisfied customer but a repeat one, too. See chapter 4 on page 112 for more details on specific actions to take after a sale goes through.

- **Thank them for their business.** Always, always, *always* follow up with a sincere thank you. Depending on what you're selling, that might be with an email, a phone call, or even a handwritten letter. It's a basic business courtesy that goes a long way and lets them know that you value them.

- **Keep talking to them.** This may be as simple as asking them to sign up on your mailing list so that you can (periodically) keep them up-to-date on new products or services. Or you may have made a sale of a complex business software that will require ongoing conversations and maintenance, in which case you'll be in touch with your customers regularly. This is a fantastic way to build  relationships and trust, so make sure you are always on top of things. As their business expands or you improve your product, there will be chances for more sales. Always be looking forward to when you might be able to help them and sell to them again.

- **Always take complaints and concerns seriously.** Look, some people just like to complain, and some are never satisfied, no matter what you do. But a good number of complaints have validity and you need to take each of them seriously. If a customer registers a complaint with you, apologize, investigate promptly, and work toward a solution that will satisfy them. This is especially true if you will have an ongoing relationship with them. In that case, you have to solve all problems in a timely manner. Sometimes it's beyond your control. Maybe the cook at your restaurant had an off night; maybe a waiter tripped and spilled something. In cases like this, offer the customer a free entrée or something similar if they'll come back and give you another chance. There's always the case where someone will hate you and write a negative review, no matter what you do. It's unavoidable. All you can do is apologize and wish them well.

- **Ask for testimonials.** If you are delivering a great product or service, it's OK to reach out to your customer base and ask for their opinions, whether that's in the form of online reviews or a personal testimonial: "If you like our service, feel free to leave us a review on XXXX, it would really help us out, thanks!" Maybe you'll offer them a "How was your experience?" survey. Just be sure to ask permission for any quotes that you may get back.

- **Don't forget the importance of word of mouth.** It's also fine to ask your satisfied customers to tell their friends. Invite them to tweet about it, brag about it, whatever they want to do. A referral bonus is another great way to get people involved, if it suits your business. Tell your existing customers that for each new person they bring to you as a new customer, you'll offer the existing one a 20 percent discount on their next purchase (or whatever is suitable for what you are selling). It's a great way to get them involved with you again and keep their interest in your work. And there's a decent chance it will bring you more business.

This is the idea behind some sites' partnership agreements, such as that offered by Amazon. If someone buys your product by clicking through an existing customer's site to come to your Amazon page, that customer gets a small bonus. So, they're getting rewarded for advertising you, and you get to keep then dialogue open with them.

[ CHAPTER 3: ]

# MAKING THE SALE AND CLOSING THE DEAL

You've prospected, you found your targets, you've reached out, you've got some interest, and now you might be able to make a sale. Argh! Help! What do you do?! Fear not, this chapter will give you a lot of practical advice on finding the best customers from your target group, and moving everything from that point onto the final sale. Get ready to learn all about making the sale and closing the deal!

# FOUR WAYS OF IDENTIFYING YOUR MOST LIKELY CUSTOMERS

From your list of targets and prospects, you'll still need to identify those who are most likely to buy from you. Even the ones who are interested are not necessarily going to be in that category, so what can you do to narrow it down even further? Here are some ways to identify those who will likely become your actual customers.

1. **Develop customer profiles:** These are especially helpful if you are selling to other businesses. You will likely have gathered some of this information during your research phase and entered it into your database (see pages 35–37). It's always good to review and update this information and keep it as current as possible so that you know whom you'll be contacting if and when you reach out to them. If you are selling to general public, you can solicit additional information, but it's important to be ethical and allow them to choose what they want to share with you. Surveys are useful both for feedback and for demographic information, things like age range, gender, income, occupation, where they live, and so on. Again, this information should be given voluntarily, and you must commit to not sharing it. But you can use what you do have to gain further insights into who in that group would be your best and most likely future buyers.

2. **Ask yourself why.** Why do these customers want to buy what you're offering? What about your product is a good fit, based on the research you've done? Once you have narrowed down profiles and given yourself real answers to what the appeal is, you'll need to review your own products again . . .

3. **Review what you sell.** Over and over, you'll need to do this. When you have a good idea of who your most likely customer base will be, it's necessary to return to your products and services, and see what will be the best fit for whom. Who among your targets will most benefit from what you offer? Are some benefits better than others for some groups? Do some people or businesses need more of one thing and less of another? Which features among your offerings are most likely to attract new customers? Just as importantly, which will possibly turn them off? Is something you're selling more geared to repeat customers? How will you focus on them? You may need different strategies for new and repeat customers.

4. **Target your ads and outreaches accordingly.** With this refined information in hand, you'll be in a better position to target specific messages to specific audiences. Do they respond more favorably to one message than another? You can try the A/B method of selecting two versions of a message to go out and see which one gives you the best response. Always remember that you're trying to drill down to the best possible match, so that you'll be more likely to bring in people who will actually buy.

> **"It is not your customer's job to remember you. It is your obligation and responsibility to make sure they don't have the chance to forget you."**
>
> **—PATRICIA FRIPP**

# FIVE METHODS TO FIND THE DECISION-MAKER

If you are selling to businesses, you'll undoubtedly have to go through more than one stage to get to the process of selling, much less closing the final sale. There will be one or more decision-makers along the way who can say yes or no to you. That's just the way it is. How do you navigate through this sometimes frustrating process? Remember these tips.

1. **Remember that it may not be the person you think it is, no matter what their job title says.** Different businesses will have different decision-makers in different places. The one saying yes to you might be a vice president at one company, but a project manager in another. For a small business, it may be the owner. So don't be put off by titles and don't try to find them based only on what they say they do.

2. **Ask.** As simple as it seems, sometimes just asking who signs off on purchasing decisions can get you the information you need. A quick phone call to your target business might be your best bet.

3. **Use your network.** An extension of asking, see who is already in your network that might be able to provide you with useful information. If you have a colleague at a company you'd like to approach, see if they can find out your best contact (and offer to do the same for them in return should they ever need it, of course!).

4. **Research the company.** A lot of information might be right there on their website, though again be mindful that different businesses give different responsibilities to differently titled people. Note especially things like how long someone has been there. If there are two people with similar titles and responsibilities but one has been there for two years, while the other has been there for five, the one who's been there longer is probably a better bet as the decision-maker. Also look at their backgrounds and qualifications, if these are listed (LinkedIn may be very useful). You can make a reasonable educated guess based on these criteria.

5. **Use LinkedIn and other online material.** Programs like LinkedIn Sales Navigator are designed to make your job easier. It states that it can "target the right buyers, understand key insights, and make your outreach personalized." It's available for free trial as both an individual and at a company level. Other online services such as Hunter, Prospect.io, ZoomInfo, and Voila Norbert are all great resources for finding contact information and directing you to the people you need to reach with a lot less hassle.

> **"Pretend that every single person you meet has a sign around his or her neck that says, 'Make me feel important.' Not only will you succeed in sales, you will succeed in life."**
>
> **—MARY KAY ASH**

# PRACTICE EVERYTHING! FIVE TIPS

> You don't want to go into any sales situation cold and unprepared. While there's no way you can possibly anticipate everything that will happen (and something will happen that you didn't think of!), the more you can be ready, the more you'll look and feel confident about the whole thing. Practice doesn't make perfect, but it does make better, so commit to getting better!

1. **Have a script.** Just as with your cold calls, write down the points you want to cover and the way you want to say them. This will obviously vary a little from customer to customer, but having a template that you can modify will make the whole process so much easier.

2. **Speak your script out loud.** This is crucial. Just reading it over and over won't do you any good, even if you do memorize it. You have to hear yourself, listen to where you're putting your emphasis, how fast you're saying it (you'll tend to speed up when you're nervous), and what your overall tone is. The more you can make this sound polished and articulate, the more professional you'll be.

3. **Read your script to others.** Get honest feedback from friends and colleagues, and make sure that they point out the good and the bad. They may hear things in it you don't, or recommend cuts or additions. It might not sound as good as you think it does, but you won't know until you run it past them. Practice and try again until they give you the thumbs-up.

**4. Practice a sales situation with others.** Now get
one or more friends to role-play the part of a buyer. See how
the conversation goes, what objections they raise, and what
unexpected things come up. Have them ask questions, give
you resistance, be skeptical, be bored, whatever comes to
mind. It's all a part of being as prepared as you can for the
real thing.

**5. Take in feedback and refine your pitch.** With all of this in
mind, you may find that your script and presentation need some work.
That's a good thing! It gets you that much closer to doing this for real.
Work and rework it as many times as you feel are necessary.

> **"Statistics suggest that when
> customers complain, business
> owners and managers ought
> to get excited about it.
> The complaining customer
> represents a huge opportunity
> for more business."**
>
> **—ZIG ZIGLAR**

# OPENING A DIALOGUE, RATHER THAN PUSHING FOR A SALE

> This cannot be stressed too much: when you talk with a prospect, whether by email, on the phone, or in person, you must *never* present yourself as a salesperson. Everyone is selling something to everyone else these days, and we've learned to see much of it as annoying and tune it out. You don't want to be tuned out! If you lead off with your product and how great it is, the potential sale is more than likely already lost. Do that a few times, and you'll learn your lesson. Or don't do it at all, follow this advice, and you'll get a lot further!

- **Make it about the customer.** The customer comes first. They are the reason you're having this conversation. Be courteous, respect their time, and accommodate them. You're the one intruding on their time, and you need to give them a good reason to stay on the phone or write back to you.

- **Don't overload them with information right away.** If you start off with "XXXX company is the leading provider of blah, blah, blah," you'll likely get nothing other than "no thank you," or your email deleted, lost in the ether and never answered. People get barraged with sales pitches all the time. There's probably nothing about you or what you're offering that's going to make you stand out to them until they learn more about you and get comfortable talking with you.

- **You're starting a conversation.** That's it.
  That's all. But that's everything. Conversations go places,
  and they can lead to bigger and better things. Hard
  sells get hung up on, and rightly so. Instead, start a
  conversation. Ask if this is a good time, and if not, when
  is a good time to reach out to them.

- **Focus on real benefits to them.** If they want to give you
  a minute of their time, great! You don't have long, so keep it brief.
  "Companies like yours are coming to us to [benefit]. How are you doing
  currently with your [need]?" Not much may come of it, and they may be
  happy with what they have, but you've opened a door and not had the
  phone proverbially slammed in your face. That's a start!

- **Let them take the lead.** If they want to talk to you further, they'll
  let you know. They may ask you to email them more information, or they
  may want to set up a time when you can talk more in-depth. If you're
  really killing it, they may even invite you to a short meetup to go into
  more detail about what you're selling! If it seems like all is going well, ask
  them "When would you like to meet?" rather than just "Would you like to
  meet?" By framing a meeting as a foregone conclusion, you're moving the
  conversation along.

- **Be accepting if they aren't interested.** Thank them for their
  time and ask if you can send them information anyway. They may keep it on
  file for future reference, and it's not at all impossible that you'll hear from
  them six months down the line, when their needs unexpectedly change.

# SETTING UP A MEETING: FIVE PIECES OF ADVICE

You've got their attention, and they may want to meet with you? Awesome! So what do you do? Well, don't get overly excited; the enthusiastic puppy look won't be a good one. Instead, do these things.

1. **Agree on a time and date.** Simple and obvious, but you need to make sure that you are meeting according to their convenience, since you are the one imposing on their time. If they're willing to take fifteen minutes or a half hour of their undoubtedly busy schedule, then you have to go with the times they propose. You just have to.

2. **Agree on a place.** It may be at their office, it may be on neutral ground (perhaps a nearby coffee shop). Rarely will it be your own place of business unless they happen to be in the neighborhood anyway, but by all means, if that works out, go for it! Just make sure it's some place you can both easily get to.

3. **Exchange contact information.** Again, obviously, but make sure that the phone number or email you're using right now is your best option. They may give you a cell phone number instead of a company phone number, for example, so that you can text if anything comes up. If the meeting is more than a day from now, confirm with them beforehand either on the morning of the meeting or the day before. Things come up at the last minute.

4. **Make sure you know what each other looks like.** This sounds silly, but if you're meeting in a coffee shop or other public area, it helps to know whom you're looking for! A quick description of your appearance or what you'll be wearing should be enough, or you might even consider connecting on LinkedIn or other social media where you have photos. You might have seen their photo on their company website, but they may not have seen yours. Send them a link, if you have one (just make sure it's a recent and professional photo, not something from your college partying days!). Anything to make the moment of finding each other a little bit easier will do.

5. **Expect that sometimes the meeting will be postponed.** Things come up at the last minute. It's disappointing, but rarely has anything to do with you; it might even be you who has to do the postponing. Just send apologies and reschedule. If they are interested now, they will likely still be interested in three days' time or a week. If for some reason, they keep postponing, it may be a sign that they are reluctant to meet, but don't know how to communicate that with you. If you keep getting put off, it's OK to gently ask if everything is fine on their part.

# TEN WAYS TO MAKE A GREAT FIRST IMPRESSION

The meeting is set, you'll be there, ready to talk, ready to make a new connection, and maybe ready to intrigue them with what you have to offer. So make sure that you show up and give the best impression you can, because you won't get a second chance. Here's how.

1. **Dress nicely.** Make sure you've showered, groomed, brushed your teeth, and are wearing clean and appropriate clothes. This sounds painfully obvious, but you'd be astonished at how often it seems to go wrong. What you actually wear will depend on the nature of your business and theirs. If your normal work look is casual but theirs is more formal, go with more formal. You want to meet them on their level. It never hurts to overdress a little.

2. **Greet them with a smile and a handshake.** Look them in the eye, smile, be friendly, and offer your hand as you introduce yourself, saying, "Nice to meet you"—or whatever seems most appropriate. Be aware that handshake styles do vary from culture to culture. While the West prefers firm handshakes, clients from India and the Middle East often see that as a sign of aggression. Adjust your behavior accordingly.

3. **Be mindful of body language.** Sit up, don't slouch (remember what you were told as a child!), don't cross your arms (it can transmit defensiveness), don't act like you're sitting on your couch at home bingeing on streaming services. Make regular eye contact without staring or being creepy, and give them your full attention.

**4. Turn your phone off.** Unless you may be needed for an emergency, you can live without it for the duration of the meeting. Whether or not they do the same thing is irrelevant. It may be that you want to take notes on a tablet or laptop, but let them know that's what you're doing.

**5. Go in prepared.** Take the time to research and really learn about your prospect, what they are doing, what they might need, what their goals are. You want to feel like you know a decent amount so that they don't have to explain everything to you from scratch.

**6. A bit of small talk is fine to start off with.** This usually happens naturally and is a good way to put you both at ease. Maybe you have something in common, or maybe you can chat briefly about the weather or the local sports team. Anything that gets a cordial conversation started is fine. If the prospect's business has done something that impresses you, lead with that. A genuine compliment is a great way to kick things off!

**7. Let them lead the conversation.** When you do get down to business, remember that you're there to listen and to learn. Don't hit them with a hard sales pitch. Take notes, and find out what it is that they are looking for.

**8. Be prepared with your own material.** When the time comes for you to talk about you, be prepared (remember, you've practiced what you're going to say!) and also have all supporting materials. Whether it's brochures, reports, or case studies—whatever puts you in a good light— have it all prepared and professionally organized. A folder or binder works really well, and is something you can give for them to take away. There is great value in being able to give them something tangible, beyond just looking it up on your website. Don't appear lazy; make the effort to impress.

9. **Be enthusiastic about what they're saying.** This doesn't require some insincere "OMG, that's amazing!" kind of thing; just take a genuine interest in what they're communicating to you, and remember that they will always care about their needs more than anyone else will, so give them the respect that shows you want to help them with those needs to the best of your ability.

10. **Be confident in your own position.** You're there at the meeting, they're giving you their time, and you're awesome, so go with that! They obviously think you're good enough that they're willing to hear you out, so be proud of that and own your accomplishments. If you have a product or service that you are putting out to the world, you're doing so because you think it's ready for the people who need it. If you second-guess, make excuses, or otherwise cast doubt on your services, you're telling them not to waste their time. If you don't have confidence in what you're selling, why should they? Of course, this doesn't means you should be arrogant! Instead, be grateful that they have given you time to show them how wonderful you are.

> **"You have to drop your sales mentality and start working with your prospects as if they've already hired you."**
>
> **—JILL KONRATH**

# IDENTIFYING AND UNDERSTANDING YOUR POTENTIAL CUSTOMER'S NEEDS

> There is no one way to do this, but it's essential if you want to get to the heart of the matter and provide a prospect with something they will want and/or need. This is an ongoing process that began when you started prospecting and continues throughout the sales cycle. Keep the following points in mind.

- **Why does this prospect need you?** What is it that they are lacking—what is their pain point, as some call it? How can you meet that want or need, and why are you uniquely suited to do it?

- **If they have specific needs, ask about them.** Especially if you are presenting something in a face-to-face meeting, be sure to ask about any special problems they are facing. They may have hidden needs that you don't know about. And they may ask how you can best solve something that you hadn't yet anticipated. Being able to think on your feet in these situations is important, and it's a skill you can develop over time. At the very least, you can offer to get back to them about a specific problem once you've had the chance to analyze it; just make sure you actually do it!

- **Recognize the different kinds of needs.** Customers will have any number of needs, but it's up to you to know what they are. Here is a list of common customer needs, both in the general public and in businesses.

You should be able to see how what you're selling fits into these needs and how it answers them:

- **Price and value:** Is what they're buying worth the money? Are they getting what they paid for, and do they feel like it's good value for money?

- **Function:** Does it work the way it's supposed to? Or does the service deliver what was promised?

- **Experience:** Do they feel good about the sale? Or do they feel cheated or ripped off?

- **Design and ease of use:** How easy it is to use? Software, a new phone, a new tool . . . they all need to be useable and user-friendly. Of course, some products have a learning curve, but can the customer make a good start on it, and will it hold their interest even if they have to commit to learning more?

- **Necessary information:** Do they have everything they need to get started (manuals, instructions, FAQs)?

- **Reliability:** Does it work? Is it going to break down? Does it have a warranty and for how long? Is the service delivering what it says it will?

- **Quality of the sale:** How competent is the seller or sales team? Are they knowledgeable or just winging it? Does the buyer have confidence in the product and the seller based on their sales presentation?

- **Quality of service:** How does the buyer behave? Are they attentive? Do they listen to customer concerns and make an effort to be assuring? Do they value the customer?

- **Quality of communication afterward:** How accessible is the seller? Do they offer support and help, and if so, is it readily available? Do they make the effort to stay in touch and see how the buyer is doing, offer updates, and keep in touch?

Understanding these needs is crucial to your future sales success.

# ASK, ASK, AND ASK SOME MORE! BUT ONLY THE RIGHT QUESTIONS

When you're having a business meeting, it's important to ask many questions of your prospect. You need to know as much as possible to make sure that your product or service is the right fit. They likely won't mind you taking a bit of a deep dive into their problem; it shows you are sincere and committed to getting to the bottom of it. Asking the right questions at the right time will help move the sale along and give your prospect confidence that you can take care of their needs. Here are some questions to keep in mind during an initial meeting and beyond.

- Can you tell me more about your business?

- What's a typical day at your office [or other workplace] like?

- What are your business goals for [whatever period]?

- What is the main issue you've been dealing with?

- What's not working for you right now?

- Why do you need to get this issue dealt with now?

- What strategies have you tried with it so far?

- Has anything been holding you back in addressing this issue?

- If you could solve this challenge, how would that help your business?

- How much would it mean to you to be able to solve this issue?

- If you have a current provider, what are you hoping to change if you work with us instead?

- If this issue is not addressed, what will happen?

- How long do you think it will take for this issue to be resolved to your satisfaction?

- If budget were no obstacle, what would you change or implement about your business?

- If we move forward, what would you expect from us?

- Are there any others you'd like me to speak with?

- When can we schedule another meeting?

> **"Most businesses rise or fall not because of the product, but the people."**
> *—STEVE CASE*
> *(COFOUNDER OF AMERICA ONLINE)*

# CREATING VALUE FOR WHAT YOU SELL: IT'S MORE THAN JUST ABOUT PRICE

Price is only one factor in what you're selling. An important factor, to be sure, but it shouldn't be your only focus, because it won't be your customers' only focus. As we've seen, we really do buy for more reasons than price, and there are many ways to create and show value that are not money-based. Here are some of the key ways to engage in value selling.

- **Once again, ask whom your product or service is for.** The ones that want it or need it are much more likely to value it, and cost will be less of an issue if they have genuine interest.

- **Identify exactly what purpose your product or service serves.** Yes, you've almost certainly done this, but go back again and check in. Knowing just what it solves goes a long way toward you getting a sense of its value beyond its price.

- **Identify everything of value that your product or service brings.** It probably satisfies many wants and needs. Take the time to list them all and you may be surprised. The more problems it solves, the higher its value will be in the minds of prospects.

- **Know your own value.** Know your value as a business and the value of what you are selling. If you don't value your own products, why should a potential customer?

- **Does your brand communicate value?** Does it? Do you already have a reputation for excellence? Fantastic! If you are still developing this, it's something to keep in mind. Brand loyalty will bring back customers who will see what you offer as valuable. Customers who are dedicated to the iPhone will always buy the latest version regardless of cost, because they value the brand more than the sticker price. The value is that it comes from Apple.

- **Don't discount things like impulse buys and sentiment.** If your customers are largely in the general public, there can be many reasons why they buy (see page 20). Look at what you offer and see how it may fit into those reasons. Gifts and impulse buys are a key component of sales, and if they factor into your benefits, then by all means point that out. Advertisements do this all the time: "This makes a great gift!" (especially at the holidays) or "Buy now, while supplies last!" (a limited-time offer makes it feel more rare). Obviously, this practice is less likely if you're selling to large corporations, but even there your customers need to feel good about the transaction. Never discount how important that can be!

# IT'S ALWAYS ABOUT BENEFITS, NOT FEATURES

**To be blunt, nobody cares that your new software took seventy million hours and a team of dolphins with PhDs to develop, and has a fantastic new integrated interface that scans the blah, blah, blah . . . It's amazing how many websites offering large-scale software or other services start right off on their home pages with ridiculous industry jargon and features. You scroll through the front page (if you have the patience) and still don't know what it does by the end of it, and don't care. And then you close that window and never go back. Don't do this.**

Your potential customers want to know what you can offer them, and that's all. If they're really interested, they might read about the specs on page seven of your site. Sure, have that information available, but don't waste people's time with it. Consider the details to be like credits after a movie. Some people will be very interested, but most will probably leave before they're finished (unless it's an MCU movie, so you *need* to see the after-credit scene!).

To be fair, feature-driven sales and marketing do exist, and can be very effective, but they generally rely on the trust of a well-established brand. Car companies can exploit this very well, if they have loyal customers who come back every so often and want to know what the best new features of this year's car are. Apple is great at listing features, too, selling all the bells and whistles of the new iPhone, rather than focusing only on how they can benefit customers. They already have a loyal fan base that knows the benefits, so Apple can proudly list what's new in each new version, which itself becomes a kind of benefit for those eagerly awaiting the next must-have upgrade.

But for the rest of us, benefits are probably the best way to go when we want to hook in new customers. Here are some reasons why you should normally choose to highlight benefits and how to do so.

- **Features are essentially talking about yourself.** You know that annoying person at the social or the party that won't stop blabbing about their work, what they've done, or the awesome project they just finished. After about twenty-three seconds, you've already tuned out and are looking to make a quick escape. And that's exactly what "feature talk" is like. You're bragging, and it comes across as pompous, and everyone is fed up with you right away.

- **Benefits are essentially talking about others.** You know how great it is when you're talking with someone who's really interested in what you have to say, or maybe they offer some useful advice or insight that you hadn't thought of? It's great to feel valued and appreciated! Well, that's what benefits are like. Telling prospects what's in it for them is a great way to capture their interest. The only way, really.

## Then do these four things:

1. **Make a list of all of the features.** Go ahead, do it. Features are not at all a bad thing; they are in many ways the building blocks of your entire product. Great features mean you have a great thing to sell, whether that's beautifully designed software or a law firm with some of the best legal minds in the area. Be proud of your features!

2. **Identify what each feature does.** What is its purpose? Why is it there? Does it need to be there? Is it something that you need to tell others about, or is it a background function?

3. **Now identify those features that provide potential benefits.** This is the key point: all those features you have are fantastic, but they have to do something for a prospect. Some will be more obvious than others. Some features work in the background, and that's fine. But others will be on the proverbial front lines, and that's what you want to highlight. Figure out concrete, real-world ways that these features can benefit a customer.

4. **Now emphasize those benefits without the extensive details of the features.** Tell your audience what's in it for them. Give the details that you need to, but don't get bogged down in them. Your focus should always be on how the customer benefits. It's fine to have a laptop with a huge and fast hard drive, but it's much more important to explain to buyers what that huge and fast hard drive will let them do. The details and specs are secondary except to those that really want them.

In the end, as the saying goes, "features tell and benefits sell."

> **"Give them quality. That's the best kind of advertising in the world."**
> **—MILTON S. HERSHEY**

# EIGHT STEPS TO PERFECTING YOUR PITCH

When the time comes, you want your pitch to speak for you, your business, and what you're selling. Having the perfect pitch is not the same as practicing saying it out loud. Instead, it's having the right information in that pitch to be persuasive. There are certain key elements to a good pitch that will give you a better chance of persuading a customer to buy. This list is a good start.

1. **Emphasize the value of what you offer.** This should include a short statement: "XXXX helps [targets] with XXXX by doing XXXX, so that they can XXXX." After that, it's OK to include some more details about what you do, as long as they remain customer-focused. Adding some personal information about how and why you came to be selling what you're selling can be good, too. People like the human-interest aspects of a story. Your intent is to build rapport and a real connection. Be enthusiastic and that enthusiasm will likely catch on.

2. **Give attention to your prospects' problems, with the message that you have a solution.** Highlight what they're going through. Show that you've spent time researching their problem. You understand it and you sympathize, but guess what? You also have a solution! Be sure that you address the concerns of each decision-maker if they are present, or if they have raised specific questions or objections in their absence.

3. **Offer real solutions.** Make sure that the solutions you propose are specific, and not just general "we can help" kind of offers. Get into some detail about what you actually can offer that will address the issue. Also, don't overwhelm them with too many options. You want to address specific problems with specific solutions tailored to those problems. And importantly, be detailed but don't be boring! You want to hold their attention, not send them to sleep with minutiae that they won't care about. Keep things as simple as they can be made to be, and don't confuse your prospect.

4. **Back up your claims.** It's all well and good to say you have the answer to their dilemma, but where is your proof? Before they commit to buying anything from you, they're going to want that proof, so have it in abundance! This can and should be in many forms: testimonials, reviews, case studies (these are especially good, since they offer real-life examples of how you helped others), data, relevant research, and whatever else you have that can make your case and back up your claims. Show them how you've fared against your competitors, and if you don't have that data, get it first. You need to be able to demonstrate why you're the better choice. If you're not doing as well as your competitors, of course, you'll need to find other benefits that you can offer that make up for it.

5. **Offer benefits beyond just those that solve their problem(s).** These incentives are especially good in your early days, when you may have fewer testimonials, less brand loyalty, or are still trying to make a name yourself. Things like money-back guarantees, free ten-day trials, additional products or services added on, and much more, can all be added on to sweeten the deal and show that you take your prospect seriously. **Important note:** Be aware that in certain business situations, offering free gifts can be seen as a bit awkward or even unethical, depending on the situation. This is also the case when dealing with businesses in some foreign countries, so do your background research first, and take a bit of care with what you offer beyond the usual guarantees (which, to be honest, you should be offering anyway!). You don't want to be seen as bribing your potential customers!

6. **Be ready to answer any and all questions.** As we've said, you have to know your product or service and its benefits inside and out, especially as they relate to this given prospect. They can and will ask you many questions, so answer every one as fully and clearly as you can. If you honestly don't know the answer, promise to get back to them and follow through on it.

7. **Make sure you have the next steps mapped out and give them a clear call to action.** The hope is that your pitch will impress and they will be ready to take things to next level. If they do, great! But make sure that you are ready to move on to the next phase. You don't want the embarrassment of looking like you haven't thought it through! If they say, "Great! So what's next?" and you're there stammering or fumbling, it's not going to make a good impression. You have to be ready to jump at the chance they've just given you. Be prepared and professional at all points in the sale. Give your prospects all the options they need to move things forward.

8. **Follow up, follow up, follow up!** After the meeting or presentation, *never* just leave your prospect to think about it and get back to you when they're ready! Always have a plan to follow up on your meeting. You don't need to be a nuisance about it (and don't want to), but make sure that you're still in the front of their minds. You might want to arrange a follow-up call at the end of the session, or agree on another meeting to discuss taking things to the next level. Whatever you do, you need to be proactive to keep the sale moving forward. Don't rely on them to take the next step, or they just might not.

# ELEVEN THINGS TO REMEMBER WHEN CREATING AND PRESENTING A SALES DEMO

> If you're giving a presentation to a group of people at a company interested in buying from you, you'll need to be well prepared and have your act together. This is not the time for flying by the seat of your pants! You already know that you need to highlight the benefits that you will bring, but what about the presentation itself? How can you make the best impression and what tools do you need? Here are some things to start with.

1. **Remember that your presentation is about your customer, not about you.** You're selling yourself without selling yourself. Always focus on what benefits you are offering, not your own accomplishments.

2. **Decide which formats will best suit your presentation.**
   PowerPoint slides, videos, photos, actual demonstrations (say, of software or a product) . . . all of these might be things you want to include.

3. **Write out your script beforehand.** This should
   be a no-brainer, but you don't want to be improvising in
   front of a potentially important client! As with calling and
   prospecting, write it out and rehearse it extensively.

4. **Have an agenda.** Set out everything that needs to be said, all the
   topics you'll cover. This can be a useful handout for the attendees.

5. **Grab them from the start.** You need to start strong. If you haven't
   gotten to the point in the first thirty seconds, you're probably going to
   lose the sale. The details can come after you've got their attention.

6. **Discuss their needs.** They're here to learn how you can help them,
   so keep that as the focus.

7. **Demonstrate how what you're selling can help them.**
   Use whichever formats seem appropriate to you, and show how your
   product or service addresses their specific needs, not just needs in general.

8. **Keep it brief enough and don't overwhelm them.** A half-
   hour presentation will bore everyone senseless. Take only the time you
   need and be careful not to give them an information overload. Again,
   practice this on others first to get a good sense of timing and content.

9. **Answer all questions to the best of your ability.** This
   requires that you be fully prepared, of course, and also prepared for the
   fact that someone may throw you a question you can't answer. Promise to
   get back to them as soon as you can and follow through with that. This is
   also a good time to answer any objections a client may have. It's a good
   idea to watch the faces of your audience throughout your presentation to
   see if you can sense resistance at any point. That's likely to come up in the
   Q and A.

10. **Have literature available for takeaway.** Hard copies (in binders, for example) are great to hand out at the end of the presentation or even at the beginning, if you'd like them follow along (but be sure that their attention is on you instead of having their noses in the books). This is where you can go into more detail with things like case studies, testimonials, and other supporting literature.

11. **Set a call to action.** You've done your part, and now it's time for them to do theirs! Summarize your presentation and make it clear what the prospect needs to do next to move the process along. This includes information about their level of commitment, what they can invest in terms of time and money, and so on. Give them a clear overall picture, and invite them to take the next step, whether that is another meeting, submitting the plan to higher-ups for approval, or maybe even moving toward the actual sale.

> **"A mediocre person tells. A good person explains. A superior person demonstrates. A great person inspires others to see for themselves."**
>
> **—HARVEY MACKAY**

# SEVEN WAYS TO OUTSHINE YOUR COMPETITION

It's very likely that you won't be the only one selling what you're selling. In fact, it's almost guaranteed. Sorry to say, but it's true! So, if you're competing with others to grab the attention of desired clients and customers, what can you do to make yourself stand out? Why should someone come to you, rather than your competitors?

1. **Don't focus on negatives.** Attacking your competitors, telling your prospect how bad they are or how poor their product is, will *not* work. It makes you look petty, unprofessional, and there's a very good chance it will get back to them. If word gets around that you like insulting people and businesses behind their backs, it's pretty much the end. If you'd do that to a competitor, who's to say you wouldn't do that to a client?

2. **Study your competition.** That being said, you need to know about your competitors and what they offer. Study them, read testimonials, get other feedback, buy their product if that's an option, learn about their customer service, and just get to know them. The more you know what you're up against, the better you'll be able to position yourself when it comes time to present what you have, and you'll be able to come up with ways that you can do better. If a prospect says, "XXXX does it this way, how do you do it?"—you'll be prepared.

3. **Always bring value and respect.** You must put your customer first at all times. As we've advised throughout this book, it's about what you can give, not what you can get. Always be focused on the prospect's needs, and work hard to deliver the best value and service to them. Consider offering discounts and other bonuses. As your brand and reputation for excellence grow, more people will remember you, and will seek you out.

4. **Present yourself professionally at all times.** Look good, present well, have your literature and info edited to perfection and designed professionally. Don't skimp on any of this, because the impression you make will most definitely influence your prospect's decision on whether or not to buy from you.

5. **Try to think ahead of your competition.** What is it that you can bring that's unique? What can you anticipate about your customers' needs that they might not? Maybe the customer will have specific needs a year from now that you can foresee and start to address now. Let your prospects know that you're in it for the long haul, not just the quick sale.

6. **Try to offer unique things, but don't rely on them.** You may be able to offer something a bit extra that your competitors don't. That's great, but don't use that as the sole talking point for why they should buy from you. You need to offer a whole package that is great throughout. If they're only buying because of a gimmick, they may resent it later.

7. **If a prospect chooses your competition instead of you, ask why.** If you don't make the sale, it's fine to conduct some market research into what happened. What was it about your competitor's offering that made it more appealing? Learn what it was that gave them the edge, and work to correct it in the future so that you can deliver a better service or product.

# REDUCING A CUSTOMER'S RISK

Buyers are naturally wary at any time, whether it's the single customer in a store or the large corporation that needs new software. Everyone is cautious with their money and won't likely just throw it at you because you tell how great you are. That would be nice, but alas, it rarely happens. How can you set a buyer's mind at ease? Here are some ways.

- **Back up everything you say.** It's not enough to make bold claims; you have to prove your words. Reviews, testimonials, and demonstrations are all great ways to show that you can walk the walk. They are the social proof that your product has been field-tested and has been proven to be a winner.

- **Offer warranties and guarantees.** These are standard, which is good because they exist for a reason. You need to be able to show that you have so much confidence in what you're selling that the prospect has an easy opt out if something goes wrong. A money-back guarantee or a pledge to repair something free of charge for the first year show that you stand by your sale 100 percent and put the customer first. That's a powerful selling point.

- **Offer free trials.** Like a guarantee, this allows a prospect to take the product for a test drive. Giving a week to try out the software, a free consultation, or a trial jar of a new strawberry jam are all ways that you can show your potential customer what they'll be getting. It puts their minds at ease and makes them more likely to buy.

- **Build trust.** This is something that develops over time, but again, if you do things right to begin with and build up a reputation for reliability and customer care, it's going to reflect well on you. A good relationship with a potential client or customer reduces risk, simply by the fact that they've gotten to know you. And this is especially true going forward, when you might want their business again.

> **"If you work just for money, you'll never make it, but if you love what you're doing and you always put the customer first, success will be yours."**
>
> **—RAY KROC**

# UNDERSTANDING RESISTANCE TO A SALE, AND OVERCOMING IT IN AN ETHICAL WAY

Sometimes, you've done everything right and the customer still isn't sure. Don't worry, this happens all the time and isn't an indication that you're terrible at sales or at presenting yourself. As noted, people sometimes are just naturally reluctant to part with their money until they can be convinced that it's a good idea. Here are some points to keep in mind and ideas for helping potential customers overcome that resistance.

- **Resistance can be a good thing.** If a customer is hesitant, it shows that there's at least some interest in your product. If they didn't want it at all, they'd just walk away. But if they object, ask questions, and say things like, "I'm still not sure," it means that on some level they might be waiting for you to convince them. Resistance can be your friend!

- **Watch your tone.** Don't go into what some call sales voice. You may not even be aware that you're doing it, but try to keep your voice to the way it always sounds. You want to be professional, of course, but don't try, consciously or otherwise, to alter your tone to sound more impressive. Usually, it's just masking insecurity, and the client will pick up on it. Ask a friend to listen to you make your presentation first, to make sure you're not being overly dramatic.

- **Speak to them from a place of understanding.** They may have never used your product before, or they may know nothing about it. Tell them that you understand their concerns and want to show them why it is still be a good choice. Put yourself into that person's mind and work from there. If you knew nothing about your product, what would convince *you* to buy it?

- **Show them enough benefits.** There has to be enough in it for them to make the decision to buy. They will only buy if they are convinced of this. Are they still reluctant? Maybe you haven't shown them enough benefits yet.

- **What if they object to the price?** Maybe what you offer is a little more expensive than they want. If so, you have to lead with the quality of the service or product. It's not just about the number— it's about what they will be receiving. Something that  will last a long time or give them a much-needed benefit is worth the extra investment. Again, let them know that you understand their concerns, and offer to show how the benefits make your item worth that little bit extra investment.

- **Always be respectful.** Let the customer direct the conversation. *Never* argue with them, shut them down, or dismiss their concerns! That's a guaranteed way to lose the sale. Don't interrupt or talk over them; it's not only rude, you may miss out on hearing something important. Always let them finish before you answer, and don't rattle on with long-winded responses. Answer their questions directly and honestly.

- **Ask them if they have any concerns.** One of the best things you can do is get those objections out of the way early. By taking the initiative, you're showing empathy, and proving that you already have the answers to the concerns they're going to bring up. That could set their minds at ease right off the bat.

- **Find the real source of the objection.** It's not always what a customer says it is. By gently asking around, you may discover that something deeper is at the root. Of course, never say something like, "OK, but what's *really* bothering you?" If you communicate that you don't trust them or come off as insulting, they'll walk right out the proverbial door.

# VARIOUS OBJECTIONS AND WAYS TO RESPOND

Whether you're on a sales call, in a meeting, talking with store customers, or any other sales situation, you'll likely encounter objections. Here are some of the most common ones and how to respond.

- **It's too expensive:** Price is a genuine concern. Show that you understand that and offer to highlight the best benefits, including saving money over the long term, if that's the case. A bigger investment now may well pay off in the future.

- **I'm not interested:** This one is tricky, because it's also code for "go away," so you have to be careful about how you respond and not get pushy. Tell them that you appreciate how they might not be interested in something they know nothing about, but if they'd be willing to give you a couple of minutes of their time, you might be able to demonstrate how this could be of value to them.

- **It's too complicated:** Are you selling software, phones, or complex machinery? Assure them that the product comes with full instructions and that you have a support staff on hand and ready to provide any assistance they need (if you indeed do have this!). Yes, the item may have a learning curve, but you can help them through it, and they'll find that once they get into using it, it may not be as difficult as they thought it was.

- **I don't have time:** Does your product, in fact, help people to save time? An upgrade to software or a phone, a new and better vacuum cleaner . . . loads of items can save time. Be creative about what your item can do to help give a customer more of their precious time back. You may be surprised at how many ways it can save someone time that you hadn't thought of.

- **I want/need more information:** This is a good place to be, because it shows that they haven't rejected your offer yet. But they're still not convinced, so you need to get them there. Make a counteroffer to give them a brief talk or demonstration that will show them in a short time much more than just sending them information could. Of course, it's also important to follow up with additional information if they want it.

- **I'm already happy with the one I have:** Ugh, this seems like a bad one. They're already using your competition and everything is just fine. You may feel like there's nothing you can do in this case (brand loyalty and all that), but don't give up quite yet. Maybe they're really not all that happy with what they're getting and are looking for a change. Emphasize how your item or service is different from anything else out there, but be prepared to back it up! This means that it really *does* have to have some new and special benefits and features that the competition's doesn't have.

# FIVE TIPS FOR DEALING WITH COMPETING BIDS AND PROPOSALS

> Unfortunately, in many sales situations, from securing a big contract with a multinational company to selling your services as a freelancer, you'll be competing against others for the same prize. You know you have a great product, but you not only have to convince the buyer, you have to convince them that yours is better than the others who are bidding for the same contract. It seems like extra work and stress, and it can be. But there are strategies that can help give you the edge.

1. **Make sure you are capable of the job and can start right away.** Obviously, you need to be able to deliver on what you promise. If you go into a bidding situation and you're not able to deliver, it's going to look very bad. Make sure you can handle what they're asking from you.

2. **Watch out for lowball bidders.** Say you're offering a service that will cost $40 an hour. But some jackass sweeps in and offers to do the same service for $18. This kind of undercutting sucks and actually damages your industry, because it cheapens it. Unfortunately, many are so obsessed with getting the bid or making the sale that they don't care. This is especially true if they are a new business trying to build up a client list. The problem with this strategy is that, while it may work for a while, you'll start getting a reputation as being cheap, and when you want to raise your rates, it will be more difficult. If you have

a valuable product or service, sell it for what it's worth, not what you think people will pay for it.

3. **Reacting when someone lowballs.** Be ready for it and counter with the value that you bring. Whether it's a portfolio, case studies, testimonials, a list of genuine benefits, a chance to try out the service or product, jump right in and show how just going for the cheapest option isn't always the best choice. Can you prove that your product will save them money in the long run, if they make an initial higher investment? Then do it! That's the kind of thing that serious buyers want to hear.

4. **Choose whom you bid with carefully.** This may seem obvious, but some companies and clients are just trying to see who they can get for the cheapest price. These are almost always a waste of your time. If you've done your research, you should be able to weed out the companies that want a cheap deal versus those who are seeking something of value. A quality client shouldn't balk at your quote, and if they do, they may not be a good fit for you anyway.

5. **Be careful about offering discounts to sweeten the deal.** It's OK if an introductory discount price is already built into your package, but be careful about giving up too much just because someone has underbid you. You could end up giving away more than you want to get the client. And again, if what you sell has value, you shouldn't need to chip away at it to impress someone. Quality clients understand this.

# HOW AND WHY CLOSING HAPPENS

There's something amazing about closing the deal, shaking hands, signing the contract, getting going on the project. It's a wonderful payoff for your hard work and proof that you've done the right thing. Here is some information about this mysterious and semilegendary event.

## A sale happens when several factors converge . . .

- **Their need matches what you're offering:** They have a want or need, and sure enough, your product or service is the perfect solution for it! If you've done your background work, you've narrowed down your targets to the ones most likely to want what you have.

- **The timing is right for their need:** Their need is happening right now, and your solution is available right now. It's a perfect match!

- **They believe that your offering has value:** You've shown that what you're offering is the right solution for them. They believe that they will get real value from buying it.

- **They trust you:** You've developed a rapport and a relationship with them, even if it's only briefly. They believe that you are honest, aren't trying to rip them off, and want what's best for them.

- **They have the ability to pay:** All of the above factors are crucial, but the customer needs to be in a position to buy, or the sale still might not happen.

# DIFFERENT WAYS TO CLOSE

- **Time sensitive:** "Buy today only, and get an additional 20 percent off!" "Only five left and they're going fast!" "We can only keep this deal around until Wednesday." Each of these offers puts a gentle pressure on the buyer to commit now. If they don't, they'll lose out on something great.

- **Give something, get something:** Customer: "Can you offer [add-on] as well?" You: "Yes we can, if you're ready to sign the contract today." The idea is to make a concession to something they want in exchange for speeding up the sales process. How much do they really want it, and will they agree to buy right now if they get that something extra?

- **Remove something, get something:** If the customer is resisting, especially over price, offer to take away one or two small benefits and make the sale at the discounted price, and see if they'll go for it, or if they decide that they actually do need those extra benefits, Again, how much is it *really* worth to them?

- **The summary:** Review everything you've told them to keep it fresh in their minds. Emphasize everything they'll be getting and how much they will benefit. The idea is to put it all in front of them, like a benefit smorgasbord, so they can see what's included in the price. This can have the effect of nudging them into agreeing to the sale.

You might use one or more of these in combination. Or you may devise your own particular forms of closing. The idea is to put some gentle pressure on the prospect to agree to the sale, without them feeling bad or pressured. You always want both sides to go away happy!

# WHEN THE SALE FAILS (AND OFTEN IT WILL)

> Sometimes, no matter what you do, the sale will fall through. A lot of the time. Maybe most of the time, especially at first. This is normal, this is natural, everyone has gone through it, and it still sucks. It's especially disappointing if it's a potentially big sale or if things were going well. Why do some promising sales just not go through?

- **Price concerns:** This is probably the number one reason. The customer or company thought it over, and decided that they couldn't afford it at this point in time. There's not too much you can do about this, since they have the authority on how much they spend. They didn't feel they were getting enough value for money, or they did but it was  just out of their budget for now. There may be some room for negotiation when this happens, but don't give the farm away chasing after one client.

- **Objections from other decision-makers:** You may have impressed the people in the meeting, they seemed interested and enthusiastic, and they wanted to move forward. But they may not have been the only decision-makers. Sometimes these processes are reviewed by higher-ups who have the final word. Maybe a vice president looked it over and killed the deal for any number of reasons that you'll never know. Maybe the CEO just issued a freeze on spending for the quarter the day after you made your pitch. Maybe the Human Resources department looked it over and said it wouldn't work for what they need. You may never know exactly why the sale failed, unless they tell you. And many times, they'll be courteous enough to do so.

- **Bad timing:** This reason often goes along with pricing. Maybe they can't afford it right now, but that doesn't mean they won't be able to at some point! Maybe they feel their business isn't big enough yet, but they have room to grow. Maybe the current buyer doesn't want to try out anything new, but ends up leaving and being replaced in six months. Being in the right place at the right time is crucial.

- **Going with a competitor:** This one hurts, but it happens. For whatever reasons, they decided that your competition offered a better deal, a better service, or met their needs in more ways than you can. Ouch. All you can do is live and learn, and commit yourselves to understanding what it was about the competition that made it more appealing, so you can be better prepared next time. Of course, maybe your competitor will royally screw things up down the line, and you can be ready to jump in and replace them! You can always hope . . .

> # "Success always demands a greater effort."
> —*WINSTON S. CHURCHILL*

# COPING WITH REJECTION (AND GETTING USED TO IT)

We all hate rejection, whether in business, getting into a preferred college, or, worst of all, in our personal lives. Thankfully, when it comes to business, we can probably not take it personally, unless we really did something to screw things up! If you've tried your best and the sale still fell through, you're going to feel bad, but it's very likely just a professional decision on the part of the prospect.

Unfortunately, rejection can come at any time during the sales process, from the initial call, to the first meeting, to a day before closing the deal, and that's just the cold, hard reality of it all. Unfortunately, a good number of your rejections will come early on, which can be very discouraging. All it takes is an hour of nos on the phone from your top prospects, and you'll feel ready to pack it in and hit the bar, or binge a streaming service and eat large amounts of junk food. Happily, getting a lot of nos up front can be a blessing in disguise, because it moves you forward to the ones who will be more open, and it gets you used to the process so that you can learn to deal with it.

Here are some thoughts on being rejected.

- **It probably isn't personal. Really.** Again, if you're making cold calls to busy people, there could be a hundred different reasons why they say no, and probably none of them have anything to do with you. If the sales process has started, we've already seen how it can be disrupted along the way. Again, it has nothing to do with you.

- **Rejection happens more often than it doesn't.** Don't let it be a surprise when you hear no. It's the norm, and it's just the way business works. No matter how great your product or service, there will always be a large number of people (maybe even most) who aren't interested. And that's OK.

- **Always act professionally.** When they tell you no, thank them for their time. Getting upset or argumentative is the best way to ensure never being able to do business with them. They may not need this product at this time, but what about later on? What about a different product? Always keep the lines of communication open.

- **If it seems appropriate, ask why.** They may just give you some excuse to get rid of you, but they may also offer you some insights that can help you refine your next call or presentation.

- **Vent to your friends and coworkers, not your prospect!** Maybe they rejected you hard. Maybe they were even a little rude. You can be angry, but never at them. Go rant about it to your best friend over drinks or share your story with coworkers (but even here be careful, so that negative words don't spread around). You may have colleagues that are in similar situations. Offer to get together and share your worst rejection stories. You may even end up laughing at them!

- **A no may still be an opening.** But don't be pushy about it! Maybe they don't need what you're selling right now. Maybe they're happy with their current provider. These kinds of reasons are very common, but that doesn't mean they will always be the case. Other sellers go out of business or fail to keep up, or the company outgrows its current situation.

It's fine to keep them on your contact list and even offer to send them some literature. If they agree, they may file it away for future reference. Offer to check in again with them in six months. If they're absolutely adamant that they don't need you, then it's probably not going to work out anyway.

- **Get back on the horse.** One rejection, two, even twenty . . . these are not indicators of future success or failure; they're just par for the course. Going in with the idea that you'll most likely hear no is a good place to start from, and takes the sting out considerably. But also know that each no is a step closer to a yes, and that persistence pays off. By all means, learn from the nos and refine your pitch and your strategies, but don't give up!

> **"Successful and unsuccesful people do not vary greatly in their abilities. They vary in their desires to reach their potential."**
> —*JOHN MAXWELL*

# CHAPTER 4

# AFTER THE DEAL

The sale has closed! Awesome! This is a big deal and not something to just take lightly. Especially if it's your first big sale or even any sale (you've opened a shop, and your first happy customer has just walked out with a purchase), it's going to feel great and give you a boost of confidence going forward. But after the sale, your work is not done, not by a long shot. What happens next? This section will give you insights and tips into what you should do next, from showing gratitude to cultivating long-term and repeat customers. After all, you want that great feeling to continue, don't you?

# THE IMPORTANCE OF GRATITUDE AND COURTESY

Manners matter. You've been on your best behavior throughout the sales process, so why would that change now? In fact, you should strive to be even more courteous, because now your customers have placed their trust in you and you have to deliver. Fortunately, it doesn't take that much effort, and a little really does go a long way.

- **Say thank you and mean it.** This can never be stressed too much. Your customers are very likely why you're even in business. Without them, you wouldn't be. Showing your gratitude, whether at the sales counter, at the end of a freelance gig, or when you've supplied something to a major corporation, is essential.

## Reach out in the way most appropriate to your business.

- **For other businesses:** An email might be fine for a company representative, but you can do better. Send them a handwritten thank-you note in a nice card. Think about it: How often do you get personalized messages in the physical mail these days? Probably not very often! Imagine the impact that would make on you, and then think about how well it might be received by your new customer. You're deepening the bond between you by telling them that they matter. It's a simple gesture, and yet so effective.

- **For customers in the general public:** If they sign up on your mailing list, an email thanking them for their purchase is quite acceptable, especially if you make a small offer with it. Give them a thank-you gift, say 15 percent off their next purchase. It shows that you value them and want them to come back for more.

 • **Follow up regularly with your business clients.** You want them to know that you're thinking about them. We'll discuss this process in more detail later in this chapter.

- **Follow up regularly with your clients in the general public.** If they've joined your mailing list, you'll want to keep in touch on a regular basis, but not so much that you get annoying! We'll discuss some great ways to do this later in this chapter.

- **Don't forget to congratulate yourself and your team!** You worked hard to get where you are. Whether you worked by yourself or in a group, you've put in the hours and gotten the results. Remember to thank yourself and everyone involved. A celebratory lunch, dinner, happy hour, or day out is totally in order!

# WHAT IF THE CUSTOMER IS UNHAPPY? TEN STEPS TO TAKE

You want your customers to be completely satisfied with their purchases. It's even better if they are delighted with them! But sometimes, no matter what you do, something will go wrong. Maybe your product will fail to work for them the way they want, maybe they have second thoughts, or maybe they're just difficult (unfortunately, it happens!). What can you do to address the problem and propose solutions?

1. **Listen.** First and foremost, the best thing you can do is listen to their complaint. It's critical that you understand the problem so you can work to fix it. It seems simple, but a customer who feels heard might begin to feel valued again. Even if their complaint seems unreasonable to you, give them the chance to tell you about it. Unhappy customers are usually very honest, and if there is something wrong, it can be a great way to learn about it and ensure it doesn't happen again.

2. **Apologize, accept responsibility, and mean it.** The simple act of an apology can do wonders. Not "I'm sorry you feel that way," but "I'm so sorry this happened to you; let's discuss it."

3. **Don't react and disagree immediately.** We tend to get defensive when we are being criticized, and we want to strike back to protect ourselves. As tempting as this reaction might be, don't do it in a complaint situation. Let cooler heads prevail.

4. **Try to be on their side.** "Let me see what I can do for you" is a good stance to take, because it shows that you're reaching out to meet them halfway.

5. **Ask them for their help.** "What can we do to make this right?" is another great way to approach the problem. You're seeking their feedback and making them a part of the solution.

6. **Speak to them in person.** If they send an angry email, get on the phone and talk to them directly. If they phone you with the complaint, make time for it then and there, unless it's absolutely impossible to do so, in which case, offer to get back to them ASAP. Direct contact is a good way to calm tempers and keep the situation reasonable.

7. **Have someone higher-up speak to them.** If you are a business with multiple employees, have the CEO or a VP get in touch with the customer to hear them out and offer apologies. Being heard by the boss will definitely help them feel valued.

8. **Don't ignore complaints.** This should be obvious, but if you get a reputation for not caring, customers will drop you. Or they'll say bad things about you online and in the real world.

9. **Be very aware of negative feedback.** Think about when someone tweets a complaint about, say, poor airline service with no resolution and tags the business. Suddenly hundreds or even thousands of people can see the complaint. And how long does it take for that business to respond? If they're smart, they'll do it very quickly! They now have to do damage control to keep their reputation from getting worse. Don't allow your business to get into that situation to begin with. If it does happen,

offer a public apology and commit to making things right for them. Be seen as being proactive and caring.

10. **Accept that some customers will never be satisfied.**
Sometimes, no matter what you do, someone will just be spoiling for a fight, hurling abuse, or otherwise making your life miserable. This is likely more the case with sales to the general public, but it can happen anywhere. There's really not too much you can do about this, and the problem may not even be you. Offer them what you can (a refund, a discount, whatever seems appropriate) and wish them well. Understand that you do not have to put up with bad behavior. If a customer becomes abusive or threatens you, you can have this person removed from your store, your office, or wherever you conduct business. If the police need to become involved, so be it. Your personal safety is paramount, and you should never feel bullied or afraid if someone wants to take it out on you because they didn't get exactly what they wanted.

[
**"You are what you repeatedly do. Excellence, then, is not an act, but a habit."**

—*ARISTOTLE*
]

# UPSELLING AND CROSS-SELLING: WHAT ELSE CAN YOU DO FOR THEM?

Once you've made the sale, you have the potential to have a loyal and ongoing customer. These are your people, and you want to cultivate great relations with them. One of the best aspects of this situation is that you now may have the opportunity to sell them other things that you offer or that are related to the product they've bought. If they trusted you once and are happy with the results, there's a good chance they'll trust you again. So what can you do?

- **Cross-selling:** At the time of the sale, there may be other items that you could include in the package as an incentive: that new laptop might include a discounted pair of headphones or a deluxe case. This is known as cross-selling and happens all the time: "Would you like fries with that?" is basically cross-selling. If you sell related products and services, it's fine to make those known to the customer at the time of purchase; just don't be pushy!

- **Upselling:** If your customer already has a certain product or service of yours, they may have the option to upgrade it to a premium or platinum version for increased benefits. You see this all the time with "Gold Memberships" and "Executive Privileges" and so on. Do they want all the bells and whistles? They can have them from you, for the right price!

## Seven ways to sell more:

**1. Research your customers' needs for other matches.**
Whether you're selling products or services, there may be other things you offer that would be a good fit for them. Be honest about it; not everyone will need something else, so try to narrow down the list of clients to those who may have a genuine want or need.

**2. Create case studies of customers who have used your service or product successfully and happily.** These are great when you want to offer those extra features to another client. If your prospect can see that others have been satisfied with the upgrade, it's more persuasive.

**3. Talk about the future with them.** Find out what their short- and long-term goals are. How can you fit into those? Will they have a greater need for one of your deluxe services next year? Put a word in their proverbial ear.

**4. Demonstrate need.** If you can show them how this would bring even more benefits to them, it's going to make a strong case for why they should buy in. In this case, need is more important than want, so analyze their situation carefully to assess why this upgrade is something they need to make.

**5. Offer a trial.** If you want more of their business, offer them a chance to try out your higher-tier or adjacent item and see if it's a good fit. This is a great way to entice potential new users from existing clients.

6. **Offer a discount.** This can be time sensitive, such as a chance to try it out before a certain date. It gives the deal a mild sense of urgency and encourages them to jump on it right away.

7. **Be wary of jumping the gun.** With upselling, be a bit careful about jumping right into making more sales pitches soon after the initial purchase. This is especially true with big business transactions. Let your customer get a chance to know you and your product, and get comfortable with it before you start hawking more things to them. You don't want to come off as pushy or desperate.

> **"If you can't make decisions and build relationships, you won't have a job in the future."**
>
> **—MORRIE SHECHTMAN**

# NINE WAYS OF CULTIVATING RELATIONSHIPS WITH YOUR CUSTOMERS

How you treat your existing customers in many ways will determine how successful you will be. You want to be there for them in the long term and change one-time customers into repeat customers. Here's how to build those relationships into strong bonds that will serve you both in the long term.

1. **Check in regularly.** After the sale is complete, checking in is important. If your client is a business that you hope to sell to again or keep a relationship with, it's absolutely crucial. But even with retail sales and general public business, you need to be available to them if they have any questions, comments, or complaints.

2. **Communicate.** Always have your door open to them and let them know that they can contact you at any time for any reason. Make yourself easy to contact.

3. **Make sure your customer feels valued.** During and after the sale, you always want your customer to know that you appreciate their business. They are why you do what you do.

4. **Make sure your customer is happy with the sale.** This is a part of checking in and is essential. If they leave the store elated but have

a problem the next day, it's still your problem. Always try to exceed their expectations in everything that you do.

5. **Solicit feedback and input.** Your customers' comments and observations can be vital to your improvement. Never fear to take their advice on board.

6. **Respond promptly.** This is vital, especially if there is a complaint or concern. Never give them the runaround or make it difficult to reach you. If they have a complaint, face up to it and listen (see page 115).

7. **If something is wrong, fix it.** No exceptions (unless they are being inappropriate and rude, see page 117). Your commitment to making things right will go a long way to repairing and maintaining trust. It's inevitable that problems will come up. Be ready when they do.

8. **Show them you're thinking of them.** Send a card at the holidays, pass along an article they might be interested in, refer a client to them, give them a special customer-only deal. Just little things now and then to let them know they're on your mind.

9. **Consider mutual advertising that can benefit both parties.** Rather like testimonials, if you have a client that is a business doing its own great things, it's a sure bet that they're busy marketing and advertising, too. Would it be to your mutual advantage to co-advertise? If you have sold them a product or service that they love, it might be worth brainstorming ways that you could do a mutual ad highlighting both of the businesses' accomplishments. This may require some digging, back-and-forth conversations, and research to see what will benefit you both, but it's a great way to get each business more in the spotlight, since you'll be sharing each other's audiences. This is sometimes called joint-venture marketing or advertising, and it's a great strategy to expand your audience.

# CULTIVATING RELATIONSHIPS WITH THOSE WHO REJECTED YOU (THEY MAY CHANGE THEIR MINDS!)

This may seem odd, but just because you haven't made the sale or secured the client doesn't mean they are lost to you forever. Far from it! Circumstances change all the time. Many a freelance guru will tell you that if you reach out to a potential client who says no, keep them on file anyway. It can and does happen that if you periodically remind potential clients that you exist and are still available to serve them, they will reach out to you eventually.

- **The timing may not be right.** The client may not have the budget, or they may have another provider, or any number of other reasons for saying no. But that no may be only for right now. Things change in the business world pretty quickly. A company may experience a sudden boom and outgrow their current needs, or your competitor may screw things up and get dumped (you can always hope!). Are you ready to step up and remind the client of what you can do?

- **The person making the decisions may move on.** Sometimes someone rejects your proposal for whatever reason, but six months later, they've relocated to another company. The person who replaces them? Maybe they want to add in new ideas and are willing to hear what you have to say. Never discount the idea of new blood bringing in change.

- **You can still learn a lot.** Inquiring as to why they say no can be very helpful to you in fine-tune your approach. Also, in getting to know them better, you may discover they have other needs you weren't aware of. Wouldn't you like to be on the receiving end of a call or email three months after a no that says they may need one of your other services instead?

- **It can only help your reputation.** Being available to interact with a potential client can put you in a very good light. Obviously, you don't want to spend valuable time and money on someone who will never hire you, but reaching out occasionally to check in, especially if you offer a bit of free advice (a tip, an article), can present you as helpful and trustworthy.

You don't want to spend a lot of time and effort impressing people who don't have any initial interest; you're better off going after the ones who do. But keeping tabs on potential clients and checking in once in a while is a nice strategy to have in the background.

> **"You may be disappointed if you fail. But you're doomed if you don't try."**
>
> **—BEVERLY SILLS**

# SEVEN TIPS FOR GETTING HONEST FEEDBACK

Feedback is essential to your growth as a business. You want to hear everything, good and bad, that your customers have to say, because it's the only way you can learn and progress. Customer surveys are pretty common, but they're not always effective. People may get busy with other things, or they're just not that bothered about responding to you, even if they're happy with their purchase. In fact, they're more likely to give you feedback when they're unhappy, which won't give you a fair distribution of answers and might just be depressing! So how can you ask for feedback in ways that will actually get a response?

1. **Determine what it is you need to know.** Be more specific than just "How did we do?" Generalizations are fine, but they may not tell you much, and they're not very inspiring for those giving the feedback. Questions like "Did the XXXX aspect of our product work as well as you wanted it to?" will give you clearer answers.

2. **Include a thank you and maybe an offer.** You should always thank them for their business, of course. But if you want some feedback, consider adding a little bonus in. If they fill out the survey, they get 15 percent off their next purchase, or, even better, enter them in a quarterly contest to win a $50 gift card. Be creative. These kinds of enticements are a great way to give something in exchange for valuable information.

3. **Make it personal.** If you can, address them by name and include your name, too. Then you are a person asking another person a question, not a machine compiling data.

4. **Be specific.** Don't ask, "Were you satisfied with your transaction?" Instead, ask, "What worked for you, and what could be improved?" This way, you're soliciting their opinion in an active way. And pretty much everyone likes to give you their opinion!

5. **Make it easy to provide feedback.** Customers are not going to take time to click through an extensive website searching for your feedback form, unless they're really angry about something. And making it hard to find is only going to make them angrier! Let them know how and where to give their feedback and make the form easy to fill out and submit. If you offer a phone number, be sure to clearly state the hours of availability, and be sure that someone is ready to answer their call. Remember how much you hate phone queues, so do as much as you can to make wait times minimal!

6. **Accept all feedback, good and bad.** Of course we want to be told that we're wonderful, but sometimes we hear things we don't want to. Sometimes you can brush them off, but sometimes you'll gain real, valuable insights into what you're doing wrong. See page 115 for more on how to deal with unhappy customers.

7. **Understand that you will get conflicting reports.** Someone may love a certain thing you do, while another person may hate it. This is normal and unavoidable. Investigate both for what might be truths and what might just be opinions. If a majority of your feedback is weighted one way or another, you'll have a better sense of what you need to do or improve.

# SIX PIECES OF ADVICE FOR GETTING AND GIVING REFERRALS

Referrals are a fantastic way to expand your prospect list and numbers of potential clients. If a client is happy with your services and recommends you to their colleagues or other businesses, it's a golden moment that you are fully allowed to savor! These are especially delicious when they are unsolicited, but it's also possible to ask your customers for referrals and not feel creepy about doing it. Here are some guidelines.

1. **Know what kind of referrals you want.** It's important that you narrow it down. You have target demographics, so make sure that anyone sent to you fits into those. It does you no good to have to field calls and emails from people and businesses that aren't a good fit. If you ask for referrals from your customers, set specific parameters, so that you're not wasting their time.

2. **It's fine to ask for referrals at the right time.** Asking a happy customer if they'd mind telling others about you is not too imposing or forward. Many will be fine doing so. Just don't make it the focus of your sale, and always make sure that they know it's optional.

3. **Use positive feedback as an opening.** The same request can apply if you get a good response or review. If the customer or client has taken the time to communicate how good they think you are, they probably won't mind recommending you to others.

**4. Don't expect more than one.** If a satisfied customer sends another customer your way, fantastic! But don't expect it to be an ongoing thing. If they liked you that much, they'd probably be working for you on your marketing and advertising campaigns! Be gracious and happy for the referral and let that one be enough.

**5. Give as good as you get.** Do you have customers that are great clients doing great work that the world should know about? Well, here's your chance to give them a boost! If you know of someone in need of their services, by all means recommend them. You need to make sure, of course, that you have full confidence in anyone you recommend. If you send a colleague or business their way and they screw it up, it's going to make you look bad and could make things awkward for your own business with them going forward. Be sure that you trust in their quality completely, because your reputation is at stake, too.

**6. But be sure your referral partner is included in the process.** If you want to refer someone to one of your customers, make sure they know it's coming their way. Saying something like "Ask for Jim; tell him I sent you" can create an awkward situation if Jim doesn't know you're dropping his name. Ask Jim if it's OK to refer people to him, and make sure he's in the loop so that he can expect the call, if and when it comes.

# SOCIAL PROOF WITH TESTIMONIALS: FIVE ACTIONS TO TAKE

> Your new client loves you! They're very happy with their purchase! Your customer is over the moon with the new thing they bought from your store! This is all great, of course, but what can you do to leverage this to your advantage? Testimonials! When nice people say nice things about your business, it not only feels good, it adds to your reputation and your brand. It makes you trustworthy and gives future customers a chance to move away from any skepticism or hesitancy. Sometimes customers will just offer you a testimonial without any prompting, but it's also possible to reach out and ask for testimonials. Here are some ways to do it.

1. **Pick the right time to ask.** This will vary from client to client and customer to customer. Right after the sale may not be the best time, since they need to try things out for a bit. For a business client, check in and see how they are using your product or service to meet their goals. Did it work? Did it exceed their expectations? Then now is the time to ask!

2. **Remember that the personal touch is always good.** In the course of your follow-ups and checkings in, you'll be talking with one or more representatives of the client, if not the clients themselves. As you converse and gauge their level of satisfaction, you might be justified in asking if they would say a few words about how satisfied they are.

3. **Make it easy for them.** Their testimonial can be as long or as short as they want it to be. They can write it, film it, or do an interpretive dance, but let them lead the way in deciding what to say about you and how to say it.

4. **Offer a testimonial or review in return.** Are they a great client? Be prepared to say something about it! Offering to exchange testimonials is great mutual support, and can only help you both.

5. **Keep in mind that you don't need a large number of testimonials.** Having seven pages of awesome quotes may look impressive and make you feel fantastic, but, realistically, no one is going to read that many. The sheer number might be impressive, but that's about it. A few well-written, sincere testimonials that outline exactly why you are great at what you do will be better than a list of fifty five-word quotes. Focus on quality, not quantity, and get testimonials first from those who you consider to be your best and most impressive clients. Anything after that is the proverbial icing on the cake.

> **"A satisfied customer is the best source of advertisement."**
>
> *—G. S. ALAG*

# ALWAYS BE REFINING YOUR SALES METHODS

Your strategy for sales will change over time, as your business grows and your clients' needs grow and change with it. What works for you now may not work for you in five years' time, or even in two years. Being able to adapt to change is essential for your continued success. Here are some helpful tips.

- **Always be reviewing your sales plan.** Even after it's done, even when it's working, if you go back to it frequently, you'll more than likely find places that could use a bit of tweaking and improving. Your plan will change as you do.

- **Be clear about your future goals.** Where do you want to be in six months? A year? Five years? You need to keep those future goalposts in mind as you progress, and be ready to adapt. Are your plans realistic? Do they need to be modified due to unexpected changes?

- **How is your demographic changing?** If you target certain groups (and you should), what changes are happening in those groups that could affect your sales? If you appeal mainly to a younger crowd, for example, how will you bring in a new generation of customers as the current group ages out of your target?

- **How is the market changing?** You need to keep tabs on changes in the market and anything else that might affect sales. What's the overall economy doing? Can you adapt to a significant change? Many of these things will be beyond your control, but if you have some ideas and strategies in place as backups, you'll be better prepared if a recession hits or some other factor impacts your sales.

- **How is technology changing?** This is a big one, as new innovations seem to come at us all the time. What new technologies are the next hot things, and are they hot things that you can use? It can seem exhausting trying to keep up with it all, but it's essential if you want to stay current. If you offer something such as software, you'll be focused on tech innovations almost constantly. Special bonuses become expected features over time.

- **Maintain the customers you already have.** What are the best ways to keep your customers while trying to attract more? Is that even a desirable goal? If you sell baby products, you'll have a constant new influx of potential customers when the current ones grow out of your market every couple of years, so you'll never be done working to attract new customers.

Allowing your business the freedom to grow will mean revising your sales strategies from time to time. This might be hard work, but it will be very rewarding if it takes you to where you want to be!

# RESOURCES

This small book can only go into so much detail,
but don't worry if you have more questions (and you
probably will!). There's an abundance of sales-related
advice out there, no matter where you are in the sales process.
These books and online resources are great places to
get much further into detail about any topic
covered in this book.

# FURTHER READING

Here is a selection of great books on all aspects of sales. Whether you're a one-person business, working for a start-up, or part of a sales team with a bigger company, there is something here for you!

Frank Bettger, *How I Raised Myself from Failure to Success in Selling* (Touchstone, 1992).

Trish Bertuzzi, *The Sales Development Playbook: Build Repeatable Pipeline and Accelerate Growth with Inside Sales* (Moore-Lake, 2016).

Jeb Blount, *Fanatical Prospecting: The Ultimate Guide to Opening Sales Conversations and Filling the Pipeline by Leveraging Social Selling, Telephone, Email, Text, and Cold Calling* (John Wiley, 2015).

Jeb Blount, *Sales EQ: How Ultra High Performers Leverage Sales-Specific Emotional Intelligence to Close the Complex Deal* (John Wiley, 2017).

Jeb Blount, *Objections: The Ultimate Guide for Mastering The Art and Science of Getting Past No* (John Wiley, 2018).

Dale Carnegie, *How to Win Friends and Influence People* (Pocket, republished 1998).

Jeffrey Gitomer, *Little Red Book of Selling: 12.5 Principles of Sales Greatness* (Bard Press, 2004).

Jeffrey Gitomer, *The Sales Bible, New Edition: The Ultimate Sales Resource* (John Wiley, 2015).

David Hoffeld, *The Science of Selling: Proven Strategies to Make Your Pitch, Influence Decisions, and Close the Deal* (Tarcher Perigee, 2016).

Tom Hopkins, *How to Master the Art of Selling* (Business Plus, 2005).

Mike Hunter, *High-Profit Prospecting: Powerful Strategies to Find the Best Leads and Drive Breakthrough Sales Results* (AMACOM, 2017).

Anthony Iannarino, *The Only Sales Guide You'll Ever Need* (Penguin Random House, 2016).

Keenan, *Gap Selling: Getting the Customer to Yes* (A Sales Guy Publishing, 2019).

Larry Kendall, *Ninja Selling: Subtle Skills. Big Results* (Greenleaf Book Group, 2017).

Adam Richards, *Sales: Mastering The Art of Selling: 10 Mistakes to Avoid Like the Plague, 12 Powerful Techniques to Reveal Any Hidden Objections & Close the Sale* (Independently published, 2016).

Mike Roberge, *The Sales Acceleration Formula: Using Data, Technology, and Inbound Selling to Go from $0 to $100 Million* (John Wiley, 2015).

Brian Tracy, *The Psychology of Selling: Increase Your Sales Faster and Easier Than You Ever Thought Possible* (Thomas Nelson, 2006).

Mike Weinberg, *New Sales. Simplified.: The Essential Handbook for Prospecting and New Business Development* (AMACOM, 2013).

Mike Weinberg, *Sales Truth: Debunk the Myths. Apply Powerful Principles. Win More New Sales* (Harper Collins Leadership, 2019).

# ONLINE RESOURCES

## Canadian Chamber of Commerce

From their website: "With a network of over 450 chambers of commerce and boards of trade, representing 200,000 businesses of all sizes in all sectors of the economy and in all regions, we are the largest business association in Canada, and the country's most influential." This site can be of great value when you want to learn more about the state of business in Canada, particularly how laws may affect you.

**chamber.ca**

## Canadian Federation of Independent Businesses (CFIB)

The federation offers assistance and advocacy to small businesses across Canada.

**cfib-fcei.ca/en**

## Canadian Professional Sales Association

This is a sales networking membership site (currently with over 20,000 sales professionals as members) that offers training, webinars, templates, and more. Available to individuals and teams.

**cpsa.com**

## The Interactive Advertising Bureau of Canada (IAB)

"The national voice and thought leader of the Canadian interactive marketing and advertising industry. We are the only trade association exclusively dedicated to the development and promotion of the digital marketing and advertising sector in Canada." IAB represents advertisers, ad agencies, educational organizations, and media companies, among others. The website offers a good number of resources, including podcasts, a newsletter, courses, a video library, and more.

**iabcanada.com**

# Professional Sales Academy

Headed by Shane Gibson, this site offers various courses for sales training and other resources. From the website: "Shane Gibson is a Vancouver-based International Speaker, author and B2B/Enterprise Sales trainer who has addressed over two-hundred thousand people over the 25 years on stages in North America, Southern Africa, India, Dubai, Malaysia and South America. He is known as one of Canada's foremost speakers on the topic of social media and sales performance."

**salesacademy.ca**

# Salesforce Canada

The well-known online program for CRM, the site also includes a regularly updated blog filled with useful information.

**salesforce.com/ca/blog**

# Statistics Canada

This is a great place to start when you're looking for demographic and population data. There's a lot to explore here.

**statcan.gc.ca**

# Tibor Shanto

The website of this top sales guru and coach. His blog contains regular postings of very useful material.

**tiborshanto.com/blog**

# Venture Accelerator Partners Blog

From the website: "Venture Accelerator Partners provides B2B sales, marketing and inbound lead generation services to start-ups and fast-growing organizations. Our clients range from mobile start-ups, to technology companies, to large industrial companies." The blog is a great resource with lots of useful information, and is regularly updated.

**vapartners.ca/blog**

# ABOUT THE AUTHOR

**Tim Rayborn** is a writer, educator, historian, musician, and researcher, with more than twenty years of professional experience. He is a prolific author, with a number of books and articles to his name, and more on the way. He has written on topics from the academic to the amusing to the appalling, including medieval and modern history, the arts (music, theater, and dance), food and wine, business, social studies, and works for business and government publications. He's also been a ghostwriter for various clients.

Based in the San Francisco Bay Area, Tim lived in England for seven years, studying for an M.A. and Ph.D. at the University of Leeds. He has a strong academic background but enjoys writing for general audiences.

He is also an acclaimed classical and world musician, having appeared on more than forty recordings, and he has toured and performed in the United States, Canada, Europe, North Africa, and Australia over the last twenty-five years. During that time, he has learned much about the business of arts and entertainment, and how to survive and thrive when traveling and working in intense environments.

For more, visit timrayborn.com.

# INDEX

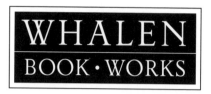

## PUBLISHING PRACTICAL & CREATIVE NONFICTION

Whalen Book Works is a small, independent book publishing company based in Kennebunkport, Maine, that combines top-notch design, unique formats, and fresh content to create truly innovative gift books.

Our unconventional approach to bookmaking is a close-knit, creative, and collaborative process among authors, artists, designers, editors, and booksellers. We publish a small, carefully curated list each season, and we take the time to make each book exactly what it needs to be.

We believe in giving back. That's why we plant one tree for every ten books sold. Your purchase supports a tree in the Rocky Mountain National Park.

*Get in touch!*

Visit us at **WHALENBOOKS.COM**
or write to us at
68 North Street, Kennebunkport, ME 04046

# TAKE YOUR CAREER TO THE NEXT LEVEL!